Black Belt for Life

Dear Kathy,

May your journey be filled with love, growth & good fortune — Best wishes always!

Black Belt for Life

A Memoir of Personal Development
and the Martial Arts

Rob Smith, Ph.D.

Copyright © 2007 by Rob Smith, Ph.D.

Library of Congress Control Number:	2007904688
ISBN: Hardcover	978-1-4257-7476-9
Softcover	978-1-4257-7450-9

All rights reserved. No part of this book may be reproduced or transmitted in any form or by any means, electronic or mechanical, including photocopying, recording, or by any information storage and retrieval system, without permission in writing from the copyright owner.

This book was printed in the United States of America.

To order additional copies of this book, contact:
Xlibris Corporation
1-888-795-4274
www.Xlibris.com
Orders@Xlibris.com
36771

Contents

Foreword 9
Preface 11
Introduction: A Black Belt's Journey 15

Chapter 1: Warriors and the Warrior Spirit 19
Chapter 2: Two True Warriors 21
Chapter 3: The Early Wonder Years 26
Chapter 4: My Induction into the Sports Fraternity 29
Chapter 5: A New Beginning 33
Chapter 6: Path of Discipline 36
Chapter 7: On the Merits of Denial and Wake-up Calls 39
Chapter 8: A Serendipity for Finding Mentors 42
Chapter 9: Love, Grad School, and the Birth of a Therapist 45
Chapter 10: Adversity and a Crisis of Faith 49
Chapter 11: The Homecoming 53
Chapter 12: My Martial Arts Roots 57
Chapter 13: Intro to Karate: Esposito Style 61
Chapter 14: The Master 63
Chapter 15: Martial Arts and Martial Living in Boston: Parallel Paths 67
Chapter 16: The Invitation 70
Chapter 17: The Test 74

Chapter 18: My Comrades 82
Chapter 19: The Long Run 88
Chapter 20: Kata Night 94
Chapter 21: Bag Night 100
Chapter 22: Technique Night 107
Chapter 23: Eddie Died Last Night 115
Chapter 24: Hell's Door 118
Chapter 25: Styx and Stones 122
Chapter 26: Living in the Fringe 130
Chapter 27: Dan Gets the Key 136
Chapter 28: Commencement Day 141
Chapter 29: Returning To Civilization: The Descent 164
Chapter 30: Life Lessons Learned So Far 168

Author's Postscript 179
Acknowledgements 181
Suggested Reading 183
About the Author 185

To my parents, Bob and Diane, who gave me everything I ever needed to thrive.

Foreword

Happiness in life is a journey, not the destination. Rob Smith's analysis of his journeys are clear, poignant, warm, and insightful. Few of us take the time to honestly review our own journey, and if we did, life would be less complex. In my life, hard work and discipline have allowed me to succeed as an engineer, a physician, in martial arts, and in a military career.

When one starts their life's journey, our bag is packed by others; our parents, grandparents, role models, coaches, teachers, and even our peers. The bag has all the tools to solve life's problems during our journey, but it has been packed by others. As we proceed in life's journey, we add some tools and discard others less helpful to us. At some time in our life's journey, our bag has been completely re-packed with our own tools to solve our own problems. This is called maturity. Hard work, discipline, honesty, morality, and good communication make this process efficient and straightforward.

Rob Smith's candor about his life's journey provides the reader with keen insights that one should apply to their own life.

Col. Arnold Scheller, MD

Preface

My name is Rob Smith, and I am a psychologist. A strange and arbitrary way to define myself, I suppose. So many times in my discussions with clients, we ponder how people identify themselves. During such conversations, I always find myself reflecting on the arbitrariness of our so-called identities. Over the course of my life, I've strongly identified myself with certain roles like athlete, student (yes, in that order for better or worse), friend, brother, son, husband, and father. It seems as though I've slipped them on and off like one tries on shoes. You wear them for a while, casting them aside for a newer version or for some entirely different style. Some fit me better than others, and some were damn hard to let go of, even when I was given the choice.

One enduring role that I have come to understand about myself as a central part of my being is that of a helper. "In the Irish family," my first generation Irish American father once told me, "there's a tradition where the first-born sons tend to be the most likely ones to become priests.[In you] I think we have our priest." This stunned me, since I've never made even the slightest connection between myself and the priesthood. In fact, I spent the better part of my youth rejecting the church. I asked way too many questions and struggled with the answers provided to me.

Somehow, though, I began to recognize the parallel between a priest's calling and my own calling to nurture and guide people. In my case, at least, this calling stems from an "enlightened selfishness." I've come to believe you cannot help others without helping yourself (whether financially, spiritually, or "karmically"), just like you can't hurt others without incurring some type of cost. When I sense that I've made a positive difference in a client's life, it reassures me of my purpose here in the cosmic scheme of things. It tells me that there was a reason for my past hurt—which allowed me to draw upon the compassion so necessary to provide a safe haven for my client's growth. It reminds me of why someone called all therapists "wounded healers."

Perhaps a more vexing part of my identity as a wounded healer involves coming to terms with my power and my powerlessness. As a psychologist, clients come to me in a vulnerable position. To address their problems, they often must admit (to themselves *and*) to me their innermost secrets—parts of themselves that they would not dare tell their parents, spouse, or closest friends. In doing so, they place in me the ultimate trust—the power to drive a judgmental sword straight through their psyche. They must say aloud what they may have feared or rejected all along about themselves. On the other hand, by treating them with respect and empathy, I demonstrate my *trustworthiness*. Having established this, I help them take a step toward trusting more in themselves.

As for my powerlessness, I have too often had to endure the humbling experience of my limits as a healer. Like an arrow released from a bow, I cannot race after my comments or actions and take them back. I've not always made the right decision in my effort to help someone. Too often, I've ignored a former supervisor's warning that no matter how compelling the problem, it ultimately is *their* problem, and I can actually do them a disservice by trying to "fix" a behavior or attitude that I deem amiss.

It's funny that as a professional in the change business, I don't change anything about my clients. In the best of cases, I merely provide the tools and a safe environment for them to take the risks inherent in all changes. With maps and compasses in hand, they must do the rest.

Another related aspect of my identity includes that of a fighter. For reasons that I will describe later in this book, this label would have seemed odd to me as a sensitive child who grew up largely in suburbia. I never would have dreamed that I would develop into a fighter—in any sense of the word.

In the martial arts, the Japanese word "Bushido" describes a way of life in the tradition of the samurai. The samurai were, of course, trained fighters, who sold their services to the wealthy landowners and merchants during Japan's feudal era. They were held in high regard not only because of their combat skills but because they followed a code of honor. This honor code often compelled them to sacrifice their own personal gain—and even their lives—for a greater good. Hence, samurais sought to follow "Bushido" or "the way of the warrior gentleman" ("bu" meaning "warrior," "shi" meaning "gentleman," and "do" translates as "the way").

Now, I'm not suggesting that I'm some kind of modern-day samurai. The idea of engaging in a real-life conflict involving swords and knives actually gives me the willies. I'm not even saying that I'm first and foremost a fighter. In fact, I have tried to make avoiding unnecessary conflicts into a fine art. I, therefore, prefer (possibly at great risk) to modify the term "Bushido" in a way that better fits my approach to life to "Shibudo".

Perhaps reversing the order of priority to the way of the gentleman warrior—Shibudo—best describes my personal style. If nobody has ever coined this term before, you heard it here first! Clever terms aside, Dan Millman in his book *Way of the Peaceful Warrior* nicely articulates what I mean by the concept of Shibudo.

Finally, in creating this book, I expand on the development of yet another layer of my identity: that of a writer. Although I've written poems, a book chapter, and some articles, writing a book reflects a greater leap of faith. Do I have a worthwhile story to tell? If I tell it, can I exorcise the technical style drilled into me during my professional training? If I invest this much time into writing a book, will someone publish it? And, perhaps most importantly, if I pour my soul onto these pages, will someone want to read it?

As I considered these questions, I kept in mind the reasons why I wanted to write this book. The main reason for writing this book at this time in my life is simple: I had to. For years, I've thought about committing to text the insights I've gained personally and professionally. People I respect and trust strongly urged me to write a book. "It'll help position you as an expert at something," some would say.

Others pointed to the royalty income I could earn without having to provide direct consulting services. Plus, book royalties could give me a chance to kiss my managed care-insurance-practice billing hassles good-bye. I even had a book publisher once call me eager to review anything I might produce. All very tempting and rational notions yet somehow still not compelling enough to prod me to fire up my PC.

Then a profound experience I had in the spring and summer of the year 2000 finally coaxed me to put pen to paper. From early April through July of that year, I undertook a highly personal challenge. My friend and karate instructor, Master Joe Esposito, had invited me to join three other students in their pursuit of his infamous black belt test. This test doesn't last a few hours, days, or even weeks—we're talking four months!

While I felt honored that Joe believed I could take on this sixteen-week journey, I also understood the gravity of his invitation. This would mean that I would have to prepare myself for the run of my life and that it was. A Christian saying goes something like, "Whatever doesn't kill you will make you stronger." There were indeed times when I wondered how I survived that journey.

Needless to say, I did. And I have since felt compelled to write about this experience—along with its inherent life lessons—to finally scratch the psychic itch that it created down the back of my consciousness.

Perhaps the most unexpected reason of all for completing this book came shortly after I started writing it: the attacks on our Pentagon and New York's World Trade Center on September 11, 2001. Along with the shock and horror most of us felt, I took that day as a sign that I can't keep putting off important goals. Such tragedies remind us of the fragility of life, and we can't keep saying, "I'll do it later."

More importantly, a key theme in this book involves coming to terms with our own prejudices, intolerances, violent impulses, and our enormous capacity to help or destroy each other. In some ways, this book couldn't have been more timely as we braced ourselves for the *War on Terrorism*.

My own personal motives aside, I hope people will benefit from reading this book in the following ways:

1. To develop insight into some keys to following the black belt path of excellence
2. To learn how to deal better with loss and other setbacks in life
3. To see how to regain trust in oneself and others
4. To provoke a reevaluation of their philosophies about the world, people, and violence
5. To gain a better understanding about what the martial arts are (and aren't) and how they can contribute to one's personal development

In this book, I touch on the metaphor of climbing Mt. Everest. The parallels between such a feat and taking this personal challenge seem inescapable. Like Jon Krackauer *(Into Thin Air)* and Anatoli Boukreev *(The Climb)*, we have four "camps" to reach before we could attack the summit—the sixteenth week of the black belt test—affectionately called Hell Week. By the time I got to the last week, we were hypoxic, weak, and on automatic pilot as we trudged wearily toward the "summit." And like anybody who has ever struggled valiantly to reach their goal, we could only stay on top of that mountain briefly before descending.

It took a long time for me to recover from my "climb," but I eventually set my sight on a new peak. If you haven't already guessed what that is, you're reading it.

My best wishes to you on all your personal journeys.

Rob Smith, PhD
Psychologist and First-Degree Black Belt, Kenpo Karate

Introduction

A Black Belt's Journey

The Parable of the Black Belt

In a hot, steamy dojo (karate school), a student has just undergone a grueling series of tests with the intent to earn his black belt. After observing his student demonstrate a solid command of many techniques and theories of combat, the master asks his student one last question before awarding the black belt, "What is the true meaning of the black belt?" Taken by surprise, the beleaguered student responded simply, "It is the end of a journey, a well-deserved reward for all my hard work." Not at all pleased with this answer, the master replied that the student was not yet ready to wear the black belt.

After a lengthy period of training over the series of months that followed, the student was once again asked the same question. To this, the student confidently replied, "It is a symbol of excellence, the highest distinction in the martial arts." Now appearing obviously aggravated, the master wasted no time dismissing his student. He told the student that he needed to return in one year.

A year later, the student returned to respond to the original question asked of him so long ago. He said calmly and humbly to his master, "The true meaning of black belt is that it represents the beginning, the beginning of a never-ending journey of self-improvement through discipline and hard work." The master paused, raised his eyes slowly, and said quietly, "Yes, now you are ready to wear the black belt and begin your journey."

This famous tale about the meaning of black belt illustrates the misunderstanding most people have about this enigmatic piece of colored fabric. Part of this confusion comes from the fact that the symbolism attached to the black belt in the above story requires a level of abstract thinking that frankly not everyone has attained. Even worse, many black belts themselves seem to perpetuate the misunderstanding of what it means to have one. Let's face it; the general public has seen some poor examples of martial artists acting in ways suggesting they only want to draw attention to themselves.

In its original meaning, earning this rank implies that the person embraces the commitment to follow the path of excellence and to embody the warrior spirit. This covenant involves the promise you make primarily *to yourself* to continually challenge yourself to grow.

Vince Lombardi, a great coach and leader of men, once was misquoted in a newspaper article as having said, "Winning isn't everything, it's the only thing." I guess it just sounded better to that reporter than what Lombardi really said during that press conference.

Lombardi apparently lamented that misapplied quote even as he lay dying of cancer. He wanted the public to know that what he said that day—and what he always tried to teach his players—was, "Winning isn't everything, but *striving to win* is." Here he emphasizes the process, not the outcome: the journey, not the destination. The end result, he trusted, would come as a by-product of his focused efforts on preparation and continued learning through experience. Lombardi had the warrior spirit and lived the lesson implied by the black belt parable.

Perhaps like all areas of life—and especially professional sports—the original spirit of the black belt's humble personal journey has been tainted by the blind pursuit of notoriety and the almighty dollar.

In his book, *The Climb*, the late Anatoli Boukreev illustrated in detail his training regimen in preparation for what turned out to be his most famous climb to the top of Mt. Everest in 1996. Boukreev had an exceptional reserve of endurance to draw upon as an elite mountaineer because of his unwavering training protocol. This never became more apparent than on May 11, 1996, when a blinding snowstorm caught several Everest expeditions by surprise. Disregarding his own fatigue, zero visibility, and unforgiving windchill temperatures, Boukreev repeatedly risked his life by retrieving stranded climbers and leading them to safety.

Prior to summiting Everest, Boukreev's training involved a process of initially just getting accustomed to the altitude of Everest's base camp, which sits at 17,384 feet above sea level. Boukreev then took his team of climbers on a systematic series of excursions that lasted nearly six weeks before they attempted the mountain's twenty-nine-thousand-foot-plus summit.

During this acclimatization and training period, Boukreev led his expedition team to four camps settled at increasing altitudes. These represented milestones that gave Boukreev a measure of his team's ability to continue the treacherous climb. It was only after they reached camp number 4 that he knew his climbers could attack the summit.

In the case of my black belt karate test—which took place between April and July of 2000—Joe Esposito, then a fifth-degree master of *kenpo* style, served as our expedition guide. Besides myself, three other students, whom I will profile later, represented Joe's handpicked team of the "climbers" he felt had the capacity to successfully complete the ascent.

The test lasted sixteen weeks. Perhaps not so coincidentally, a champion triathlete told me that this reflects the ideal training time to prepare for one of the most exhausting endurance sports imaginable. During this test, Joe takes his students through four pretests (like Boukreev's four camps en route to Everest's summit), covering a vast array of skills and knowledge. Only after successfully navigating your way past these milestones will Joe allow you to take a shot at the summit during the sixteenth and final week, which students refer to as Hell Week.

This last week of the test earned such a bootcamp-like title because of its extreme intensity. Participants can easily get mentally and physically frazzled by that point in the test. Only those lucky enough to have had no serious injuries and to have met Joe's expectations (which he never reveals completely or directly—you only know for sure when he tells you to report to the next test date) get to partake in the last week.

Nevertheless, the demands placed on both mind and body during this crucial phase of the test require all the conditioning of the prior fifteen weeks to keep your focus. To add to the drama, Joe and his black belts remind us of the stories about students who have flunked this test at literally *any* point—this includes the very *last* day of Hell Week, as four students did a few years ago.

Joe does not hesitate to remind you of this unfathomable possibility. Remember the Greek myth about Damocles? His king had him sit under a sword suspended by a single hair to remind him of the tenuous nature of the ruler's approval. In Joe's court, there would be no exceptions and no special considerations. As he told me privately one day in his office with his thick Boston accent about a prior student, "Hey, Rawb, we ah close, but Danny's the godfathah of my *son*, and I flunked him; so do you think I wouldn't flunk *you* if I thought you weren't ready to pass?"

So on these harshly honest terms, we proceeded together down a path less traveled. In doing so, we joined a select group of men and women that comprise only a handful of the many students that Joe Esposito has tutored over nearly three decades.

This book contains the formative steps along my personal journey, leading to this climb to the summit of a very meaningful accomplishment. Those not involved in the martial arts will soon understand that this test represents much more than the many movement sequences and skills on which we were tested over a sixteen-week period. The specific content of the test is actually secondary in importance from my viewpoint. For me, this test stands for one's willingness to push limits, to adapt quickly to changing circumstances, to risk loss and failure, and to grow personally.

It was an extraordinary experience—a marvelous feeling of satisfaction, triumph, and rebirth. Yet I'd had my share of personal triumphs before. It happened to me in sports, when I got married, when I completed my PhD, and when I fathered a beautiful boy named Evan (in Gaelic, this means "a gift from God," which indeed he is).

The uniqueness of this experience, however, is what I plan to share with you, along with the many lessons inherent in it. To provide the best context for why I took this path in my life, I must share some of my pertinent background.[1] You will need to know what radio personality Paul Harvey would call the rest of the story. But first, I will extend the above discussion of the meaning of the black belt by describing the difference between what people commonly refer to as the warrior mindset and true warriors. This will hopefully highlight the ideals of military service (i.e., to serve and defend) from which modern-day martial artists have emerged.

---

[1] Except where it was absolutely necessary to provide an accurate account of certain experiences, I chose to change the names and certain details of people outside my immediate circle of family and friends to protect their anonymity.

Chapter 1

Warriors and the Warrior Spirit

Maybe it all started out as an innocent metaphor, but I think we use the word "warrior" too often to describe any strong-willed or aggressive person. We call athletes warriors—politicians, business people, and even kids in some cases.

In my view, you cannot consider yourself a warrior unless you have received combat training—plain and simple. Apart from mercenaries and criminals who may also have such martial skills (known during the feudal Japanese era as *ronins*), true warriors by definition ultimately serve others. They live by a code of honor that serves a purpose reaching beyond self-interest. As such, they deserve our respect for their deadly skills and for the vital services they provide for the rest of us.

This is not to loft warriors as a superior caste of people nor to put down those who pursue a more peaceful path. Mahatma Gandhi and Martin Luther King led peaceful revolutions and clearly demonstrated their warrior's spirit without ever injuring or killing a soul. They paid the ultimate price for their causes and, therefore, hold a special place in our twentieth century history—but they were not actual warriors.

Examples of today's warriors include soldiers, prison guards, police officers, federal agents, bodyguards, and martial artists. All must prepare to perform under dangerous circumstances, executing the proper skills on demand—where errors and hesitations can make a life-or-death difference, not that most warriors *want* to die or to witness the death of others. But they must accustom themselves beyond an intellectual level to the reality that death comes as a logical risk inherent in their path.

As I implied earlier, I believe you can have the warrior spirit without ever having trained to handle occasions when someone's life might be at stake. Go to any oncology treatment center or spinal cord unit, and you'll find people of all ages undertaking the most desperate and heroic of battles. Listen to the stories of immigrant families overcoming enormous odds to develop thriving businesses here in the United States.

If a civilian can have a warrior's spirit, can a true warrior ever *lack* this attribute? I don't think so. Sure, we occasionally hear about the soldier that abandons his platoon in the heat of battle or the cop who hides in a dumpster until the gunfire stops.

At some level, we can hardly blame them for fearing for their life. Yet this defies their training and sworn commitment to serve and defend—invalidating their title as a true warrior—and indicating that these people probably should have been doing something else. The mettle of warriors gets measured on their readiness to properly perform their duty after it's no longer a drill, and the bullets start flying. Sometimes a warrior may enjoy the luxury of a second chance after freezing under fire (at the likely cost of someone *else's* life), but such circumstances tend to take a more Darwinian turn.

In the next chapter, I offer two examples of true warriors who more than met their call to service.

Chapter 2

Two True Warriors

Sergeant Alvin York

WW I's reluctant yet most decorated U.S. soldier, Alvin York grew up the eldest of eleven children in the impoverished Tennessee farming community of Pall Mall. He and his siblings lived with their parents in a two-room house. York and his father had to hunt game for their family's survival. An excellent marksman, York's father taught young Alvin how to track and shoot wild turkeys. Instead of simply blasting their torsos with buckshot, his father warned him to aim for the head—an extraordinarily more difficult target, especially when moving. This avoided wasting any meat that could help feed the family.

Helping the family with hunting and farming chores took priority over formal education, and York could only attend school during the three coldest months of the winter each year. When his father died after getting kicked by a mule, York dropped school altogether and assumed full duties as head of the family. His formal education amounted to nine months, but he would later become the consummate self-taught man.

By his early twenties, York's long work hours would lead to frequent nights of binge drinking with his best friend. After his friend got killed in a drunken brawl, however, York awakened to the self-destructiveness of his ways. Seeking moral and spiritual grounding, York became a born-again Christian.

When the United States entered World War I, York received his draft notice. Now a devout Christian, York had strong reservations about his impending duties as a soldier. At the time, he could not justify killing other people. Accordingly, he initially rebuffed his draft notice by filing for exemption as a conscientious objector. The U.S. Army denied his application.

York had the good fortune of getting placed under the command of Major Buxley, a man well versed in biblical references to the subject of taking human life. He encouraged York to reason that he may have to kill enemy soldiers to prevent the loss of even more people. York embraced Buxley's logic to such an extent that he grew to consider his impending role in the war as serving God's will to end an evil tyranny.

Having come to terms with his moral dilemma, York committed himself fully to the mission set forth by his commander and his country. Drawing from his hunting skills acquired in the Tennessee hills, York quickly impressed his superiors. In a soon-to-be-legendary battle, taking place in France's Forest of Argonne, the then Corporal York's regiment got pinned down by a German machine-gun nest positioned atop a ridge. York and a couple of his men managed to flare out and get behind the enemy line.

Finding an even higher vantage point, York had a clear line of sight into the machine gunner's stronghold. From this position, York killed several of the Germans before a group rushed him with bayonets to his left. Reportedly, he yelled at them to stop before he had to kill them. Of course, they ignored his pleading, and York killed them all with one shot each to the head—with the same stone-cold precision he used back home shooting wild turkeys in midflight.

When the battle ended, Alvin York had killed 25 German soldiers and captured 132 more as prisoners. This incredible feat led to his promotion to sergeant, a Medal of Honor, and a national acclaim as a hero when the war ended. York turned down many lucrative offers for his personal gain but instead leveraged his fame to raise money to build a school for underprivileged children from his hometown.

Although he later yielded to Hollywood's pressure to produce a film about his life (the 1941 movie, *Sergeant York*, starring Gary Cooper), he did so at President Roosevelt's urging to stoke the country's morale as they entered the Second World War. Ever-humble about his wartime accomplishments, York once said, "Instead of being remembered for my wartime heroics in the Argonne forest, I'd rather be remembered for my educational heroics in the Tennessee hills."

Lt. George E. Young

As a kid, my only firsthand experience with a true warrior involved my uncle George. I knew him mostly as a restless but caring middle-aged man who doted on my dear aunt Aggie. Over two decades earlier, Uncle George came back from World War II with medals for valor and a nervous tick that never really went away.

One of those unlikely heroes of the Second World War, newsman Tom Brokaw would have called Lt. George E. Young typical of America's greatest generation, and like so many of that era, my uncle George never sought the role of hero.

A shy yet handsome man from the perennially low-rent north end of Hartford, Connecticut, my uncle George earned the nickname Pep because of his high-energy level and diminutive stature. A lover of sports, he tried out for all the teams in school, only to be deemed as too small by most coaches.

The Army National Guard did not hesitate to select him, however, and Uncle George seemed to thrive in this environment, where he trained as a machine gunner. He earned the rank of sergeant by the time the Japanese hit Pearl Harbor, and his crew joined the 169th Infantry Division stationed in the Pacific. Uncle George never saw any action while serving in the Islands for the first two years of WWII.

Ironically, shortly after marrying my mother's sister, Agnes, in 1943, he got transferred to the Twenty-eighth Infantry. This landed him smack in the eye of the storm raging across Europe. Before the war would end, Uncle George would survive five major battles, including Hurtgen Forest and the Battle of the Bulge.

Along the way, he would see such severe casualties within his unit that the army granted him a battlefield commission promoting him to second lieutenant. He would hold his friend while helplessly watching his brains ooze out of a hole in his head sheared open by a mortar shell fragment (after this incident, the army gave Uncle George a month of R & R before sending him back into action).

Like so many veterans, my uncle didn't talk much about his war experiences. He came home from the war shell-shocked—what we now call posttraumatic stress syndrome—or a nervous wreck, as my aunt Ag would say. Like the moon, his vivid recollections shone most clearly during his sleepless nights, yet a paler version of them still lingered by day. With some prodding over time, Uncle George would open up a little of the old wounds that plagued his conscience.

Recognized by his commanders for his heroism under fire, my uncle shared with me (by then I was in my early twenties) the story of how he earned his first of two Bronze Stars: in one skirmish, it seemed that German troops had pinned his platoon down near a bridge, leaving his men exposed. Fearing for their lives, everyone just laid there as the enemy slowly picked off soldiers one by one.

Uncle George told me that he never figured out what got into him, but he recalled at some point just getting angry. Channeling his rage and fear, he sprung up and literally started kicking the behinds of his men to follow him across the bridge—which many of them fortunately did—and they went on to overtake the Germans' position.

Rejected for his small size in athletics before the war, machine gunner Pep Young played his heart out for the team that accepted him and shaped his character. He served his regiment well, and he never let them or his country down. A decorated officer, Uncle George returned home after WWII ended and took a job as a foreman at a tobacco factory—where he worked faithfully and humbly until he retired at age sixty-five.

Too young to understand the magnitude of his sacrifices, I never fully grasped why my uncle would break into tears while watching the antiwar demonstrators of the Vietnam era. My aunt told me later that "he was very proud to be a soldier and to have served his country," and that he never could accept the American public's blatant disrespect shone toward its own soldiers.

My Uncle George died shortly after his seventy-second birthday in 1988. He received a proper military burial, with everyone reflexively twitching to the crack of twenty-one guns.

Although born in different eras, York and Young came of age as our country became engaged in the First and Second World wars, respectively. York needed spiritual coaxing to serve in his role while Young always did what was asked of him. Despite (and perhaps because of) their heroic battlefield experiences, York and my uncle shied away from the limelight and generally avoided interpersonal confrontations.

Apart from their own unique personal thumbprints, these true warriors share certain similarities:

1. They all underwent training in how to fight and kill. Their skills became so well ingrained through intense training that they became second nature. They trusted these skills with their lives when under attack, and they fortunately emerged intact.
2. To acquire this level of skill, they all had to experience a training process the Japanese call *shugyo*. This refers to training in which a person gets pushed to (and sometimes beyond) the brink of collapse as a way of hardening the spirit in preparation for the adversity they will face in combat. Some describe this as a cleansing experience, paving the way for more confidence in one's ability to handle such adversity. In the military, we see shugyo training most prominently in their boot camps, but it occurs at other points in the development of a soldier. A commanding officer once confided to me that, "The goal of our training is to teach our soldiers how to respond to chaos in an organized and systematic way." In order to do this, they must constantly train to perform under duress—thus hardening themselves to better endure pain and danger. As a result of such training, these skills meld into a complex cluster of survival reflexes upon which they can rely in dangerous circumstances.
3. They each had to confront their fears and perform in potentially life-threatening situations. Ambrose Redmoon put it well when he said, "Courage is not the absence of fear but the recognition that there is something more important than the fear." This dispels the myth that brave people never experience fear. Of course, warriors must possess bravery

and the ability to survive dangerous conditions. But they don't *lack* fear—this could lead to disaster for themselves and those around them. In fact, they actually *need* a certain measure of the energy generated by their fear to sharpen their senses and quicken their reactions. To overcome the impulse to run for cover in the face of danger, they often tend to align themselves with a greater purpose that extends beyond their own lives. Defending family, friends, country, or the right to freedom can serve as a powerful tonic for overcoming fear and despair. Lieutenant Young's medal winning performance under fire in Germany serves as a case in point: initially, he got scared like the rest of his company. But then, he got mad. His anger in watching his men getting massacred flipped his switch and mobilized him into action. More recently, Army Sergeant Charles Horgan spoke about his reactions after getting shot during an Iraqi ambush. He said that he started to panic after realizing the condition of his smoldering foot. "But then my training kicked in," he went on to say, "and I started checking on the rest of my men." Of his inspiration to fight back, Sergeant Horgan said candidly, "I joined the army to defend our country, but once the shooting started, I fought to protect my friends."

4. Finally, these warriors all share a commitment to excellence in the way they perform their duties and live their lives. After returning from WWI, York read books voraciously and used his fame to develop schools for kids. My uncle became an excellent golfer and parlayed his leadership skills into a role as a factory foreman. Earlier in this book, I mentioned this continuous drive to excel (emulated in the black belt parable and in concluding segments) as a vital aspect of a warrior's mindset. U.S. Air Force Major Forrest Morgan—also an accomplished martial artist—echoes this ideal for today's modern warrior in his book, *Living the Martial Way: A Manual for the Way a Modern Warrior Should Think*. He shares the following advice from a Japanese writer, who urges us to avoid neglecting the need to sharpen our bodies and spirit:

> In an affluent society, it is necessary to purposely seek out the challenges that were once a part of the daily life of the warrior. This drive to test the limits of one's own potential is universal. (Dr. Alan Hasegawa)

As I mentioned earlier, I do not count myself among the ranks of a true warrior. A child of the turbulent sixties, I chose a different path. But as Dr. Hasegawa points out, the relative comforts that were allowed to me in my youth did not dissuade me from purposely seeking out personal challenges. In the remaining chapters of this book, I will detail the biographical experiences that led to my pursuit of the martial arts and ultimately toward becoming a black belt for the rest of my life.

Chapter 3

The Early Wonder Years

My black belt journey nearly came to an untimely end twice before I reached the age of ten. The first near-death experience came when I was two: my parents found me one morning draped over my crib, lips blue and gasping for breath. I must have gotten stuck in the railing trying to climb out for help. My folks rushed me over to the hospital in a borrowed car, and the doctors said I had pneumonia and severe asthma. They listed me as critical. But my constitution apparently would not give in, and I got discharged two weeks later.

The second time I nearly died came on a sunny summer day at a swimming hole near my home called Spring Pond. It involved one of my best childhood friends, Troy Halliwell, who lived nearby. We did everything together: lunch at school, sleepovers, and, of course, trips to Spring Pond. One day, Troy had dared me to follow him on a swim across the entire pond. I couldn't keep up with him, and by the time I reached the halfway mark, I started cramping up. Troy swam ahead, completely unaware of my distress.

I had always wondered why people bobbed up and down when they cried for help in the water. That day I found out. After I started to sink with fatigue, I vigorously pumped my arms and legs to get my head above water. This allowed me just enough time to yell for help before slipping back under. My tired limbs glowed a surreal green-yellow color as they thrashed beneath the pond's sunlit surface. Adrenaline shot through my entire body with the acute awareness that this could be the end of my young life.

After repeatedly bobbing for air and screaming for help, I could feel my body losing steam. Then suddenly, I felt a strong grip across my neck and chest pulling me upward. A lifeguard had responded to my distress call and brought me back above the water line. As he dragged my spent body toward shore, I felt the ache in my acid-laden muscles with his every stroke. I still can recall the sweet relief of the guard's timely rescue and how he made it possible for me to once again breathe freely.

TV's hero the Lone Ranger used to save people in danger every week. Those he rescued would often say that they never had a chance to thank him for his help. Well, after that lifeguard got me out of the water, I never even saw his face—much less thank him. I just walked away groggily in a daze through the crowd that had gathered by the dock. Yet, without him, my arms and legs would have eventually succumbed to the fatigue, and I would have slipped under quietly for the last time.

While I now stand six feet seven inches tall and weigh only 205 pounds, I grew up fat as a boy. In the second grade, I weighed in at 110 pounds and could proudly eat dad-sized portions at the supper table. My classmates were astounded. One day at school, my friend Mike Maloney brought his mom's bathroom scale to recess. A crowd of kids clamored around me on the playground as I stood on the scale, confirming my earlier claim about my weight.

When I got a little older, I came to understand that there was something wrong with being fat. Since I often couldn't wear the same styles as my peers, clothing store clerks quickly ushered me to the "husky" section. One year, my participation on a midget football team entailed getting routinely yelled at by my coach (who himself weighed no less than 250 pounds at six feet tall) in front of my teammates for exceeding the weight limit. I had to attend every game with no hope of playing.

By age ten, some of the kids at school developed less-than-benign nicknames that called attention to my size and physique. For example, one boy—whom I don't think I've ever truly forgiven—used to call me Tits (in recognition of my flabby chest) right in front of all the other kids at a local swimming pool. I wanted to cry, run, lash out, and scream—but instead I just took it.

As a kid, it always perplexed me how I seemed to be such an easy target for taunts, typically from older boys. I later came to appreciate that this undoubtedly occurred because of my size (besides my width, I stood five feet tall in the third grade, one inch taller than Mrs. Brown, my homeroom teacher) and sensitive demeanor.

In short, I served as a desirable target for bullies because (a) I was big, enabling them to sidestep the social no no of picking on someone smaller; (b) I was slow, which meant that I couldn't catch them, at least not on foot; and (c) basically, I didn't like fighting, which meant I would more often just put up with the harassment. But somewhere inside me, the frustrations grew.

I didn't know it then, but my experiences with bullies as a young boy would become one of the seeds of my later interest in the martial arts.

Now, I don't mean to portray my childhood as pure drudgery and abuse. Despite my occasional hassles from bullies, I had many good friends and a loving family. So I actually had many positive experiences to counterbalance some of the tyrannies of my boyhood. I just recall sometimes feeling truly confused and sad about why kids couldn't act more nicely toward each other (maybe we could say the same about why nations feel they must inflict harm on their neighbors). Clearly, I had a lot to learn about life.

Chapter 4

My Induction into the Sports Fraternity

One organized way to teach kids' life's hard lessons is through sports. In my earlier days, I loved music and drawing more than sports. I used to watch football games for the halftime show on my parents' black-and-white TV when the marching bands would take the field. Nevertheless, when it came time to sign up for peewee baseball, there I was, standing on the field with a cap and glove.

After spending the first nine years of my life sitting on my butt, I obviously had a *lot* to learn about baseball. Forever the responsible parent, my dad took it upon himself to properly usher me into the sports fraternity. One day, he took me out into the backyard to learn how to swing a bat. He wanted me to hold it properly and squeeze the bat as I swung, but I wasn't getting it. I can recall crying out of frustration and insisting that "I can't do it." "Yes, you can!" he would counter as he kept lobbing balls for me to hit. My mom wept from the back porch as she witnessed my rite of passage into sports. I'm sure it was painful to watch.

Frustrated with my failure to follow his instructions, Dad decided to intentionally hit me on the leg with a pitch. Like a dose of cold water used to revive a hysterical child, the sharp sting of that hardball converted my helpless sobs into focused anger. What started as a simple batting lesson had now become the stage for an archetypal showdown between father and son.

Without speaking a word, I wiped my eyes, resumed my stance, and awaited the next pitch. That ball seemed to float in slow motion toward me. Squeezing the bat, I stepped forward and swung as hard as I could. Then it happened: that euphoric sound when ball and hardwood connect perfectly. I barely felt the vibration in my hands as I completed my swing.

Call it an unspoken Freudian rivalry fulfilled or merely poetic justice, but that ball headed straight at my father. He hardly had the time to flinch before the ball thudded into his stomach and bounced away. Instead of getting angry, as I feared he would, my father yelled, "Now *that's* how you do it. Nice hit!"

We laughed together later as we inspected the circular bruise that had formed on his stomach. This event represented a powerful moment for me—it became a fond memory between father and son and the beginning of a lifetime love affair with sports. Besides learning about swinging a bat, I think I gained my father's respect. And I realized that, yes, indeed, I could accomplish things that seemed difficult at first glance. This would become a theme that has repeated itself for the rest of my life.

On that day in my backyard, I learned something about baseball and life.

By the time I turned fourteen, I began to shed the extra weight through the mixed blessings of puberty. Something else happened that year: I joined Coach Ron Foster's freshman football program. This year, I wouldn't have to ride the bench because of my weight, and this was the year I would go on to gain the respect of my peers for my physical skills. All the cool guys at school seemed to accept me after years of feeling like I didn't fit in with the popular crowd.

It amazed me how my simply getting involved with a school sports team could lift me out of social obscurity. All I needed to do was knock a few guys over with my pads on, suffer through mad dog Foster's double sessions, and earn a starting tackle spot. And *bam!* I suddenly found myself among the nouveau riche of the school's social scene. Even girls started to take notice of me.

Adjusting to my new role in school felt a little disconcerting, but I more than liked it; I have to admit I craved it. There is nothing quite like male affection masked by aggression. Being a part of Coach Foster's team gave me the chance to develop physically and emotionally, and it had what Mark Salzman called in his book, *Lost in Place,* that "seductive mixture of fear, violence, and male bonding" (p. 48).

The uniqueness of Coach Foster's program was that he was also the school's chorus director. That's right—the chorus director. He waved a baton—although he broke several out of intense frustration during rehearsals—and he could carry a tune.

Nobody questioned anyone's belonging to Coach Foster's choral group. This made it beyond socially acceptable to express my artistic musical interests in public. It was actually desirable for players to be in the chorus—kind of like extra credit for Coach Foster's football team. He once even made reference to my hard work ethic on the football field during a choral practice to promote such virtues in his chorus. While I recall blushing at the attention Coach Foster's compliment drew, I was flattered and proud to be in his good graces.

Later that year, I had one of those teenage male experiences that would put my newfound self-confidence to the test. While playing goalie in a pickup street hockey game at school, a football teammate berated me for giving up a goal. The player was a hothead star athlete, who owned a majority share of the popular vote at school. Handsome, multitalented, and from a well-to-do (at least for my hometown) family, Mike Maloney had been a friend during elementary school. He was the kid who brought in his mom's scale to recess back in the second grade and who used to do my math homework for me. But we had drifted apart over the years for no particular reason.

Mike's criticism ticked me off to the point where I shot something back like "Shut the f—up, Maloney; you try playing goalie if you think it's so easy!" Feeling perfectly justified and vindicated by my retort, I shifted my focus to the next face-off that was about to happen. That was my first mistake: cursing Mike Maloney out and not expecting him to retaliate.

The next thing I felt was the sting of Mike's hockey stick as he threw it at me. As I spun toward him somewhat startled, I froze with indecision about his intentions—mistake number 2. I guess if someone throws a hockey stick at you and glares at you with his fists up, he's probably not interested in inviting you to his birthday party.

Mike threw a quick right-reverse punch to my jaw that rocked my brain stem to the point of near unconsciousness. I heard bells, saw birdies, and felt a rather sharp pain in my jaw. It was all I could do to stay on my feet—though it didn't matter since the fight was over before it started. Thank God, Dr. Roberts removed my braces the year before, or my mouth would have been a complete mess.

Our gym teacher, who saw the whole incident, just kicked Mike out of the gym for the day (today, Mike would have been suspended from school for a week and possibly charged with assault); and that was probably only because the fight seemed so one-sided. I felt shocked, angry, and humiliated. I barely made it to the privacy of the locker room before crying uncontrollably.

To make matters worse, Mike later asked me in front of some other kids, "You okay, Smitty?" *Ughh!* I thought, *now Maloney thinks I'm so pathetic he has to feel sorry for me!* Naturally, I just lied and said I was fine.

I felt my newfound confidence and stature gained through my membership on the football team all but evaporate in a split-second. In the competitive adolescent male psyche, Mike's unanswered punch reflected on my shortcomings as a young man. I committed the grievous sin of not fighting back—it's okay to lose a fight, but no respect is given to the guy who takes a shot and then only cries about it.

Every time I moved my aching jaw, the jolt of pain served as a reminder of the entire ordeal. While the physical hurt only lasted a week, it took a lot longer for me to fully recover from the emotional blow. In psychologist Dr. Bill Pollack's terminology, I underwent a "shame-hardening" experience, and I clearly had not at that point sufficiently toughened up.

And yet here I need to consider mistake number 3: my taking the experience of getting sucker punched as a sign of *my* inadequacies. It never occurred to me then that Mike had the more alarming and dangerous problem. He solved arguments with his fists and had to hurt other people to feel good about himself. In my heart, I know I did not buy fully into this macho ideal. But in some ways, I did. My third mistake involved my making this experience a measure of my self-worth in the male arena.

My redemption and personal healing would come later—not on the street or on the football field but on the basketball court.

Chapter 5

A New Beginning

It happened in my sophomore year, East Catholic High School. I had a disturbing experience during that football season that may have influenced my decision to try my hand at basketball instead. A new friend of mine, Henry Jordan, started with me on the junior varsity team. We both saw a little action on varsity, but Henry seemed destined to break into the limelight as our school's future in the backfield. A tough-nosed fullback, fast and strong, Henry had a sweet disposition off the field but played intensely whenever he had his pads on.

It was a sunny fall afternoon in 1975, and the late-day shadows loomed over Danville High School's football field. Unlike most games where the chilling wind would whistle through our helmets, the air seemed unusually still that day. In a passing play, Henry stayed in the backfield to protect our quarterback.

As a defensive lineman charged in for a sack, Henry lowered his head to make the block. Upon impact, the vertebrae in his neck shattered, and Henry dropped helplessly to the ground. Just as the referee whistled the play dead, I could hear Henry screaming that he couldn't feel his legs. Something terrible had happened, and we all knew it.

It turned my stomach as the emergency medical technicians (EMTs) carefully loaded him into an ambulance. For reasons I still cannot comprehend, we actually resumed play afterward. As if this was no different than any other injury and the show must go on. Well, this was not like any other injury we'd ever seen, and we just went through the motions for the rest of the game. Not surprisingly, we lost. And Henry's life would change forever.

We also lost our innocence on that day, our sense of invulnerability. Teenagers often operate under the assumption that they will live happy, healthy lives until they get old (ranging from thirty to eighty) and die. This defensive wall of denial of our mortality tends to thin out gradually over time—if we live long enough to wake up and see what the musician Sting observes as "How fragile we are." This process evolves slowly unless you happen to watch a fifteen-year-old teammate get paralyzed right in front of you.

The entire student body walked around for weeks in a daze trying to process what happened. School officials kept us loosely informed about Henry's surgery and rehabilitation. I never saw him again until graduation day when he rode up the stage ramp in his wheelchair to accept his diploma. He got a long standing ovation. I felt tears welling up at the thought of what that young man had to overcome to graduate on time with his high school class. Henry had learned how to use that same tough-nosed intensity off the field despite and perhaps because of his paralysis.

Football season hadn't even ended when someone approached me to try out for the basketball team. I hadn't played since I was nine, but I guess the coaches saw my size and figured I couldn't be too bad. They were so wrong. Though I stood at six feet two inches and was fairly athletic, I quickly bumbled my way to the bottom of the food chain in this program. Fifteenth man on a fifteen-man team. Unlike football, basketball took more finesse than I had yet attained. "Smitty used to be the butt of our jokes in the lay-up line," my coach would later admit publicly in a newspaper article.

Something about the sting of getting razzed daily from teammates during practice stuck with me. Our varsity hoop team was highly talented, and their coach had a long-established tradition of winning state and league championships—something our football program could not boast. I decided at some point during that difficult first season that basketball would become my future.

We'll see who'll be laughing next year, I thought to myself with a resolve not unlike Alexandre Dumas's vengeful *The Count of Monte Cristo*. For the first time in my life, I would dedicate all my spare time to develop myself as a top-notch player. *We'll see*, I thought again.

The following year, I came to school having grown to six feet five inches, 185 pounds. My physical dimensions aside, nobody could recognize the player I had become when I stepped on the basketball court. Their last memory of me consisted of my dropping passes, bouncing the ball off my size 13 feet, and lofting air balls and bricks. Now I caught my passes, made my layups, handled the ball, and could dunk.

In most circles, especially among all the white guys attending my catholic school, you could suck in every other aspect of your game—but if you could dunk, you were all that. Forget the spin dribble, boxing out, and sealing off the baseline. Just slam one home, and everyone would take notice. People would constantly ask you to jam it and would stare as mesmerized as moths around a streetlamp.

I went on to start that year for the junior varsity team and went up to varsity toward the end of that season. What a powerful lesson I learned that year: if you want to become better at something, you need to have focused passion. You need to work on your weaknesses and to open yourself up to new ideas and techniques. And remember those guys who mocked you all last year? This year, they watched *you* play—from the bench! *The Count of Monte Cristo* had made his point.

It was an immensely satisfying year in many ways. Besides basketball, I sang a solo in the choral group, appeared in the school play, and I had my first serious relationship with a girl. Mary was a sweet, energetic senior whom I met in the school play. We dated most of my junior year—an eternity I guess in high school—and we both decided amicably to stop seeing each other. We stayed in touch for years afterward, and she remains in my mind as my first love. Let's put it this way: I still remember her birth date.

Chapter 6

Path of Discipline

The redemption I experienced during my junior year marked for me a turning point, a profound awakening of my warrior spirit. I had begun what the black belt parable in the Introduction referred to as a never-ending journey of self-improvement through discipline and hard work.

Although I didn't know it then, I would later employ that same determination and self-discipline time and time again in my life. For example, as a new psychologist to the Boston area—a city second only to San Francisco in shrinks per capita—I recall literally having flashbacks of my basketball workouts during the first year or two. While I toiled away at the computer and on the phone trying to develop my business, visions of my former training regimen would pop into my head.

To stay focused, I placed a Post-it note on my computer screen reminding me to "get visible." After spending thousands of hours and nearly all my savings—and losing fifteen pounds in the process—I produced an average growth rate in my practice of 20 percent over the next five years.

My practice remains filled with many interesting clients to this day because of the contacts I developed in those early years. Someone once said, "Judge each day on the seeds that you plant, not the harvest you reap." This has proven true in my personal and professional life: the most meaningful relationships I have today have come from thoughtful cultivation over long periods of time.

In his popular book, *Mastery: The Keys to Success and Long-Term Fulfillment*, George Leonard describes the path of mastery as a practice involving the pursuit of excellence in mind, body, and spirit. He emphasizes that one does not reach mastery, as one might achieve a specific capability or end point. Instead, he views mastery as the journey itself—the process by which we attain ever-higher levels of skill and character. Leonard's thoughts echo those of the Greek philosopher,

Aristotle, who believed that "We are what we repeatedly do—excellence, then, is not an act, but a habit."

In my last year of high school, my path would contain all the pressures of sports, academics, and college applications. I would need every ounce of that budding warrior spirit to confront these challenges, and it was powered by the adrenaline of my newfound hoop dreams.

The idea of playing college basketball took hold in my mind after I started receiving many letters from college coaches expressing an interest in having me play for their school. Some were even from Division I schools that offered scholarships. I had played well over the summer in camps and leagues, and I guess these coaches saw some potential in me. In my vanity at that time, I never questioned the fact that these letters started arriving even *before* I ever started a single varsity game for my high school team.

With nearly our entire varsity squad graduating the prior year, the team in my senior season fielded a cast synonymous with inexperience. That year contained a number of firsts for me: my first varsity start, my first time ever elected as a team captain, my first newspaper article with my picture on the front page of the Sports Section. This new visibility made me blush, but I felt proud and even a little bit famous (people I didn't know seemed glad to meet me, and kids asked for my autograph—rather bizarre when I look back on it now).

That year had its share of highs and lows. In one midseason game, I stumbled upon what some refer to as the zone—a performance state where I seemed to move effortlessly around the court, doing whatever I wanted offensively and defensively. I made moves that day that I had only previously seen on TV. It felt magical, but this "flow state" left me the very next game. In fact, it only returned a precious few times during the rest of my entire competitive career—part of my reason, perhaps, for my professional fascination with "flow states" as a sport psychologist today.

My last high school game took place in the second round of our state tournament. We had played poorly the whole game against an inferior team. Our head in the clouds, it seemed, we somehow managed to find ourselves down one point with two seconds left in the game. Facing elimination, our entire season and my high school playing days now hung on a miracle. During our last time out, our coach drew a play in the huddle involving a Hail Mary full-court pass to me waiting under the basket. Coach wisely chose Eddie Jones, who had a cannon for an arm, to make the inbound pass.

As everybody in the gym anticipated this strategy, the entire opposing team camped all around me to pick off the pass. Like a bad repetitive dream, I can still see Eddie launch his pass in slow motion—a frozen rope that I half-expected to tail off in its trajectory. But it kept coming toward me and my new best friends. We all jumped together as the perfectly thrown pass approached, and my arms stretched up the highest. Unfortunately, the ball ricocheted off my hands, then the Plexiglas backboard, and the game-over buzzer sounded.

Later on the team bus, Eddie, forever the wiseass, said to me quietly, "Smitty, I'm sorry I hit you on the hands." Hey, it took the Russian team three tries to pull off a similar play in the 1972 Munich Games to hand the United States their first-ever Olympic basketball loss. Still, I wrestled with the question of "Why couldn't I have caught that damn ball?" In fact, if I hung on to that ball that day the way I hung on to the guilt of muffing that pass, we would have won that game. It would take awhile for me to acknowledge my humanness and let go of my self-blame—no, thanks to Eddie, of course. Ironically, it was also Eddie who later drew my attention to a newspaper article announcing that I had made the all-conference team that year.

Although I lived and breathed basketball, my season had ended. For better or worse, this forced me to focus on my college plans. When pressed on applications to list a potential college major, I cited psychology, since it represented the only academic subject in which I had developed any strong interest. Even then, I became fascinated with the insights of pioneers of the field like Freud, Jung, Adler, Rogers, and Ellis. Unlike other subjects—in which I did just enough work to get by—I read all my Psychology in Literature class texts from cover to cover. The As I got in that class furthered my interest in keeping this area open as a potential career path.

Around that same time, I began watching the TV series *Kung Fu*, starring David Carradine. Besides his capacity to subdue the town bullies he encountered along his journey, Carradine's character, Quai Chang Cain, had a peaceful, reflective manner that captivated me. I greatly admired the combination of his fighting skills, compassion, and spirituality. Perhaps I could also identify with the restlessness he carried with him as he patiently and faithfully pursued a goal in his life; he sought connection with his long-lost brother, while I ached for a direction of my own. In any case, that character and the *Kung Fu* series opened my eyes for the first time to the mysterious world of the martial arts.

As for my college hoop dreams, it became clear to me after playing only one year of varsity basketball that I was not ready to hack it at the collegiate level. So after completing high school, I decided to attend a postgraduate year at Northfield Mt. Hermon, a prestigious preparatory school in western Massachusetts. My rationale at that time involved my needing to develop myself athletically and academically to broaden my college options.

Chapter 7

On the Merits of Denial and Wake-up Calls

In retrospect, I could have attended prep school for five more years and still wouldn't have gotten any bona fide scholarship offers. But that's what I had fixed my mind on at the time—and I wasn't prepared to let the realities of my limitations as a player sink in just yet. It must have been hard for my parents to walk that delicate line between helping me plan realistically for life after basketball while simultaneously not bursting my bubble.

The harsher truths of life would soon dispel my delusions of grandeur, but at that time, I needed to dream—to have a focus, something on which to fix my eyes on the horizon's edge of my young adulthood. But back then, if you asked me who I was, I would have answered that I was first and foremost a basketball player.

In general, I have noticed that my ability to deny my limitations has often served me well in many life pursuits. "A little bit of denial goes a long way," so the saying goes when it comes to achieving difficult goals. I have found that such pursuits require a balancing act between denying one's limits and accepting reality. However, one can block out too much and become completely unrealistic, and the results can range from exasperating to disastrous.

In his best-selling book *Into Thin Air*, Jon Krackauer chronicled the events leading to the highly publicized deaths of several climbers during a blinding storm on a Mt. Everest expedition. Of climbers in general, he writes,

> Mountaineering tends to draw men and women not easily deflected from their goals. By this late stage in the expedition, we had all been subjected to levels of misery and peril that would have sent more balanced individuals packing for home long ago. To get this far one had to have an uncommonly obdurate personality. Unfortunately, the

sort of individual who is programmed to ignore personal distress and keep pushing for the top is frequently programmed to disregard signs of grave and imminent danger as well. This forms the nub of a dilemma that every Everest climber eventually comes up against: in order to succeed you must be exceedingly driven, but if you're too driven you're likely to die. Above 26,000 feet, moreover, the line between appropriate zeal and reckless summit fever becomes grievously thin. Thus, the slopes of Everest are littered with corpses.(p. 233)

While I had a solid year playing hoops at prep school—we lost in the New England championship game to a team led by future NBA player and coach, Rick Carlisle—I found no coaches waving scholarship offers for me to attend their school gratis. Ultimately, I chose a local school with a strong academic reputation, where I knew I could play ball.

On the other hand, my experiences at Northfield Mt. Hermon gave me a rather unexpected plum: for the first time in my life, I felt smart—a couple of teachers there helped me discover that I had an intellect, which might serve me well later on in life. This realization would eventually serve as my salvation when I got to college.

My fantasies of an extended basketball career sustained a mortal blow the first official day of practice during my college freshman year. I chose to play for this particular college because they had a young and talented team, and their coach had big ideas for their program (*and for me*, I thought). A successful entrepreneur in his business career, Coach Bob Shannon knew how to make a sale—and I bought into his package big time.

The preseason went well, as I had trained hard to become a top player for my new team. I had high expectations for my future at this school, and Coach Shannon stoked the fire of this vision by saying things like, "You're gonna be a helluva player here," and "I have no doubt you will be a future Hall of Famer here." That my former high school coach joined the team as an assistant that year only further boosted my hopes for a great experience at that school.

Like so many life-altering experiences, I began practice that first day having no idea what lay ahead of me. During a routine one-on-one drill, a teammate bumped me midair, and I landed awkwardly, blowing out my right ankle. Our assistant coach would later say he heard the *pop* of my ankle from half court. The explosion of throbbing pain literally stole my breath away. It felt like napalm fire raging uncontrollably inside my sneaker and racing up the right side of my shin. I eventually forced out an "I'm okay" between panted breaths. But I knew I wasn't, and I wasn't going to be okay again for a long time.

I didn't know it then, but at that very moment, my ankle would become the center of my consciousness for the rest of my competitive basketball career and beyond. In the training room, they took off my sneaker, which had become an unwitting tourniquet after the injury occurred. The rush of blood down to my right ankle made my foot look more like a swollen cow utter. My toes looked like little stubs on the end of this fleshy, discolored ball that was my foot just an hour earlier.

The road to recovery became complicated by a change in the dynamics between my coach and I. He had a team to lead, but I grew increasingly resentful of his callousness toward my condition and his abrasive feedback style. My confidence plummeted as I struggled in vain to fight my way back into the lineup. By the year's end, my spirit had broken. Never the same player again, I felt I had lost my edge—that essential faith in oneself that all athletes need in times of adversity.

The following year, I went through the motions in practices and saw relatively little varsity-playing time. It baffled me to see guys I once outplayed regularly blow right past me in drills—it was like I knew where I needed to be, but I couldn't get myself there. It also killed me to see my coaches lose their belief in me. On the rare occasion of a compliment, the best they could muster would be that I could be a "good player" for them—apparently no longer a "future Hall of Famer."

For perhaps the only time in my life, I experienced a clinical level of depression that permeated all areas of my life. Like watching the *Titanic* slip slowly into the icy sea, I could see my hoop dreams disappearing before my eyes. In my frustration and bewilderment, I became a dissenter on the team, an insecure jerk socially, and a frustrated student. Unable to even focus well on my studies, I nearly burst into tears when I visited a professor about a poor test grade. Something had to change. As a matter of emotional survival, I sensed myself detaching from my identity as a basketball player.

Chapter 8

A Serendipity for Finding Mentors

In my life, I have had the good fortune of having encountered several people who went on to assume a mentor role for me. Somehow, I always seemed to find them when I needed support and direction. But was it just dumb luck that caused these mentors to mystically appear for me?

The answer to that question makes me think of the word "serendipity." *The Random House Dictionary of the English Language* defines "serendipity" as "an aptitude for making desirable discoveries by accident." While I know luck played a role in my finding good role models, I'm equally sure that I have had the gift of recognizing the value of what these people could contribute to my life.

With my competitive sports persona sinking during my college sophomore year, academics became my lifeboat—a kind of salvation and sanctuary from the painful losses I had come to experience on the basketball court. Thankfully, I had someone I could turn to: Dr. Pauline Murray, a professor to whom I had grown close at that time. She had nurtured my passion for psychology and for self-understanding. She saw my struggle, and she knew I needed to find my way down a new path.

Based on our conversations, I decided at some point in my sophomore year that I wanted to become a psychologist and that to climb that long academic ladder would involve my transferring to a more nationally known program in that field. Since my present school had become associated with some painful memories, the decision to leave came fairly easy to me. Looking back, the importance of Dr. Murray's contribution to my development as a person and a future psychologist cannot be overstated.

As I transferred to the University of Wisconsin to pursue a career in psychology, my serendipity came in handy once again. There can be no other way of describing how I came across the next and perhaps most influential role model in my professional life. It happened one afternoon when I knocked on the door of a professor whom I knew studied clinical psychology issues. I wanted to introduce myself and to see if he had any research assistant positions available. Unfortunately, he said he needed to attend a meeting and couldn't talk with me.

Unruffled, I noticed the open door in the next office down the hall. It read, "Daniel Kirschenbaum, PhD." Checking my roster of professors, I noted that he too was a clinical psychology instructor. As I knocked, a bearded young man sitting at his desk with long rough auburn hair and wire-rimmed John Lennon glasses looked up at me. He invited me to sit down, and I spent the next hour getting to know this man and his professional interests. Without knowing it then, I had just formed a relationship that I would treasure for the rest of my life.

Our mutual passion for athletics led to Dan's introducing me to the emerging field of sport psychology. Suddenly, it clicked for me how I could stay in touch with my athletic identity while pursuing a career as a psychologist. As a sport psychologist, I thought, I could learn more about what happened to me at my prior school. I could work to help athletes and coaches perform their best. I could show up to work with a sweat suit and sneakers on! My head spun with excitement.

My conversation with Dan lit a fire in me, more like a bursting supernova, actually. The death of my hoop dreams cleared an opening for the birth of my identity as a budding psychologist. I now had a new vision and mission on which to focus my irrepressible energy, and I couldn't wait to get started.

Dan and I would eventually publish two studies on the subject of coach feedback and its impact on how we learn and perform athletic skills (hmm . . . I wonder where I got the idea to explore that subject). Upon graduation, I was accepted into the University of Cincinnati's, Dan's alma mater, graduate program in clinical psychology. There, I could begin a new set of challenges that would hone my skills as a traveler on the path of mastery.

Before I left for Cincinnati, my dad sat me down in June of 1983 and wanted to discuss the finances associated with my going to grad school. The light from our living room window shone behind him and cast a shadow across his somber facial expression. He asked about tuition and housing costs and started to mention the need for more student loans when I interrupted him. "Don't worry about the money, Dad, I got it covered—I get free tuition, and they're gonna pay me a monthly work-study stipend." Then I just sat there and watched his face while he processed the news I just shared with him.

He looked up half smiling and said in a tone of mock disbelief, "Do you mean to tell me that all I have to do is send you a couple hundred bucks every now and then, and that's it?" My suppressed smile broke into a full grin, "Yep, that's it." Rising out of his chair, Dad jumped with fists skyward and shouted out an exuberant, "Yippee!" He seemed proud of me, and I felt proud of myself too.

Previously, I had coveted the prospect of earning a college scholarship because of my basketball skills. Beyond the status that came with being a scholarship athlete, I wanted to spare my folks the burden of having to cover my undergraduate education. Not achieving that caused me to harbor a certain sense of failure inside.

Ironically, the University of Cincinnati made all that go away when they offered me a package worth nearly $100,000 by the time I would graduate—with no student loans to pay back. I finally got my scholarship—and this one was because I was *smart*, not because I could dunk. Go figure. Maybe this served as another wake-up call. Maybe my strongest abilities existed *between my ears*, and *not* on the hoop court.

Chapter 9

Love, Grad School, and the Birth of a Therapist

Someone once said, "It is better to travel hopefully than to arrive." This makes sense in a way, since we all spend considerably more time pursuing things than actually attaining them. The important thing, though, is to love the journey because we don't always know where it will lead—or whether we'll be prepared for where it takes us.

After graduating from the University of Wisconsin-Madison in the spring of 1983, I eagerly arrived on campus at the University of Cincinnati the following fall. Just days earlier, I was saying another painful good-bye to my mother, whose propensity for painful good-byes goes unmatched. This also applies to getting off the phone with Mom—you simply cannot have a two-to-five-minute phone call with her. Since my original departure from home for school at eighteen, however, she's gotten much better at letting me drive away without throwing herself across the hood of my car.

Cincinnati's campus felt so different from UW's. Surprisingly, the student enrollment numbers were close, but UW's campus spread across a much larger area (if you forgot your notebook, you borrowed notebook paper from a classmate, as there was no way you were going to trudge two miles back to your dorm in Madison's infamous subzero winds). UC's campus had a more compact layout and had that low cost of living so important to a college student: it still blows me away that my rent for a two-bedroom, heated apartment only set me back $250 per month.

One woman I bonded with right away had come from an Ivy League school and had a cute, tomboy way about her. Amy was bright, funny, and athletic—she played on boys' sports teams in high school and could knock the stuffing out of a baseball at the batting cages. It was Amy who first introduced me to tae kwon do, a Korean martial arts system, and put a bug in my ear about trying it myself one day.

January 1985. After getting unceremoniously dumped two months earlier by a woman I had dated for several months, I came back from our Christmas break ready to fly solo for a while. Two of my best friends and I headed out for an evening of fun and dancing at a local club.

That's when I first met the woman who would later become my partner for life. Pilar and her sister had just strolled in and ordered a drink, and I simply couldn't take my eyes off of her. Concerned that someone else might ask her to dance, I leapt from my stool and made my hasty invitation. She smiled politely and declined, saying that she had just gotten here and ordered her drink. But she did say, "maybe later."

Of course, I knew she had just gotten there—she had never left my sight—but I lost all sense of timing or patience when I saw her walk in. I also knew that "maybe later" could've meant "maybe later," or "not in a million years, buddy." The uncertainty of that message fluttered in my stomach like pretest butterflies.

I walked away feeling a little like Will Ferrell's character on *Saturday Night Live* who stalks women to the disco tune that asks, "What is love? Baby don't hurt me no more." My pals teased me for my utter lack of composure, but I clung to the promise of a "maybe later."

"Later" came when my Spanish roommate, Luis, approached the bar and overheard Pilar and her sister speaking in their native tongue. Seizing the moment, I joined them, and soon after Pilar said that she was "Ready for that dance now." We closed the place, and I walked her and her sister home to their apartment. One fine good-night kiss later, and my goose was cooked. I walked home in the freezing cold, but I felt nothing but excitement over having met this person, whom I just knew was special. My serendipity struck again but this time in love.

Lofted by a strong tailwind of romance and zeal to complete graduate school, I rapidly progressed through classes and the research project that would become the basis of my master's thesis. The first in my grad-school class to successfully defend their thesis, my plan had run—to that point at least—right on schedule.

Most PhD clinical psychology programs offer a curriculum of course work much like undergraduate classes in format. Concurrently, students learn the basics of the design, data collection, and write-up of research projects. In the interest of efficiency, these collections of work would ideally morph into your masters and dissertation papers.

Strange as it may seem, grad students usually spend relatively little of their time actually practicing the art of psychotherapy while in school. For this, they must wait until they complete all their courses and begin their full-year, predoctoral internships. Such programs provide the clinical part of their training, and students typically complete them at locations outside their current school. This happens, theoretically at least, to ensure that these aspiring clinicians get a diversity of perspectives and styles within their training years.

Unbeknownst to me, back in the 80s, the University of Cincinnati was an oddity among its peers by offering their clinical students a "captive internship" program. One of eight in the country at that time, this virtually unheard of (and now extinct) arrangement enabled us to finish our supervised clinical internship prerequisite without ever having to pursue it elsewhere. Instead, we simply completed this requirement on site at UC within our first four years. All this came with the American Psychological Association's (APA) seal of approval, or so we thought—but that's another story that I'll share a little later.

As I said earlier, I sailed through my first year unscathed and even somewhat confident in my emerging skills as a therapist. This came, thanks to the marvelously supportive supervisors who worked with me at the UC Student Counseling Center from 1984-1985. I still draw upon the insights and techniques taught to me by these fine psychologists during that delicate period of my training.

One important source of reassurance and humor came from Sid Stein, an advanced grad student who had many years' clinical experience. Obviously bright and capable, you always wondered why Sid hadn't already gotten his doctorate and vacated the premises. He seemed to hate the program for dealing him some undisclosed injustice for which he so blatantly held a grudge. His view of therapists as "emotional whores" who charge clients money to "pretend" to care about their stories suggested that his disillusionment had spread beyond UC and into the entire profession of psychology.

Amazingly, this never came across as particularly discouraging to me or my fellow classmates. Perhaps we could sense that beneath his cynical exterior lied a genuinely warm and caring person who really enjoyed helping us learn the craft of psychotherapy. Sid's perceptive and at times comic insights about our clients—and even some of our professors—constantly cracked us up during supervision meetings.[2]

Like it was yesterday, I can still recall his reassuring me that I would do fine in my very first counseling session because he said I seemed good at making friends. "Forget about all the theories or trying to be like the therapists you've read about," he advised, "just treat this person like someone you just met and wanted to get to know them better."

---

[2] Sid once theorized that one of our professors, known for his arrogance, succeeded as a family therapist mainly because he managed to piss off *everyone* in the family—and that this represented "probably the first thing they had all agreed upon together in years: that their therapist was an asshole."

In what felt to me like a masterstroke, Sid linked my confidence in my personal skills with the basic tools I would need to interview my first client. It was all I needed to calm my nerves before walking into the room. A therapist was born on that day, with Sid serving as midwife—a very hairy Robin Williams kind of midwife—as he no doubt did for countless other neophyte caregivers.

Chapter 10

Adversity and a Crisis of Faith

The first of two major snags during my stint at UC came during my second internship placement. One might call such experiences "character builders," but it still sucked to have to go through this type of drama as a novice clinician. It emerged out of a strange relationship with my new supervisor, and it caused me to doubt my ability to ever become a competent therapist.

While interning at a correctional facility, I had the bizarre privilege of working with the most difficult kind of clients imaginable: drug abusers, thieves, murderers, rapists, molesters, and the severely psychotic. Some of my clients carried all these descriptors at once. Having to pass several gated security checkpoints along the way into the mental health unit, you could not help but feel a little intimidated about the kind of people with whom you would be working with. You wondered if you ever made a real difference in their lives or if they were too far gone or, even worse, you were just getting played by some psychopath for their own entertainment.

Dr. Samantha Lewis had worked her entire career in this kind of setting. A short woman with long fiery, blonde hair, she went by the masculine nickname Sam in a place that reeked of testosterone and impending aggression. Sam Lewis could hold her own there, and nobody seemed to challenge her authority. Her sense of humor reflected the sarcasm and sacrilege of her environment, and she was razor sharp in her judgment of the inmates that came through the unit.

I learned a lot that year under Dr. Lewis's watchful eye, to say the least. Two other interns and I grew quite familiar with her view of people and the world in and out of the cage in which we worked. To blow off steam, we would meet for drinks after hours to discuss cases and joke around with each other. The only one not on a student's budget, Dr. Lewis would often pick up the bar tab.

Toward the end of that year, I got a call from our clinical director. He told me he had a recent conversation with Dr. Lewis, and she apparently said she planned to give me a very poor evaluation. "I'm telling you this to give you a heads-up," he confided, "and also so you can try to be at your very best for this last month of your placement." I told him I was shocked by this news and that she had never shared with me that she felt so unhappy with my work.

The last month went by in a blur. I tried to be extra attentive to my work, all the while feeling like whatever I did would be too little too late. At the end of my last day, our secretary said that Dr. Lewis had left early. I told her that I thought of this as odd, since Dr. Lewis had not reviewed with me my end-of-year evaluation. "I'm not sure about that," the secretary said, "but I saw her put something in your mailbox before she headed out."

Sure enough, a sealed folder with my name on it sat there in my box. I said good-bye to the various staff I'd worked with the past year and then passed through the electronic gates for the last time clutching the unopened folder under my arm. Sitting down at the bus stop outside, I braced myself and tore apart the seal. I apprehensively scanned her numerical ratings and commentary.

Not surprisingly, Dr. Lewis rated my competence across the many skills I had supposedly learned over the past year at the bottom of the scale. Good thing the school's form did not provide negative numbers, as I'm sure she would have given me at least a few for good measure. Each poor rating shot jolts of panic and nausea through my stomach.

Despite my director's warning a month earlier, I could not have prepared myself for the sheer causticity of Dr. Lewis's words. Much of it has faded into the dark recesses of my memory, but her parting shot still lingers to this day-which went something like, "And I seriously hope that Mr. Smith does not become a psychologist unless he can overcome these deficits." Completely stunned, I just stared out the bus window as it chugged uphill back toward campus.

"Rob, this eval is *so* negative it actually makes *her* look bad," a friend and psychologist for whom I did some part-time work told me after reading it. Unfortunately, my clinical director stayed noncommittal—dismissing it as "a negative interaction between two people." Instead of coming to my defense, I guess he didn't want to risk losing the placement for future students. He just told me that I should write a rebuttal letter answering to some of the unfair criticisms lodged at me. I wrote the letter with the help of my psychologist friend.

It took another year of supervision from supportive professionals to regain the confidence I had lost in my abilities to help people. As I have so often done, I managed once again to find such support from good mentors and to erase the pain of my last placement.

That same year following my experience with Dr. Lewis, I had a conversation with the student who filled my spot at the correctional facility. He asked me questions about the way I was treated by Dr. Lewis—in particular, if she had ever mentioned any sexual references during our conversations. As I thought about it, she had made many comments about her sex life, pursuit of nudist retreats with her husband, and told some raunchy jokes over the year. Not especially ruffled by these incidents, I just passed them off as her colorful quirkiness.

And then I recalled a comment her secretary made about the possibility that Dr. Lewis may have been rebuffed by my not catching these comments as possible overtures. Because the notion of having a sexual relationship with her was so unfathomable, it never occurred to me that my bad evaluation might have come from the hand of a woman scorned. That she never had the guts to review her concerns with me in person lends some credibility to her losing her professional objectivity with me.

I'll never know for sure in my case, but I know that the next guy she supervised filed a complaint with the Ohio Psychology Licensing Board. Later that year, Dr. Lewis had her license suspended for what we now call sexual harassment of her male intern.

Pilar's graduation from UC's business school had a bittersweet taste because this meant her moving out of town for her first work assignment. The two-hour hike from Columbus wore her down after a while, and my not having a car left her saddled with the drive most weekends. We fought on the phone over stupid things and didn't dare do so in the precious time we had together on Saturdays and Sundays. We hung on the promise of my completing school and reuniting in the same town again.

Back on track after the Dr. Lewis's debacle, I zeroed in on finishing my dissertation. Only one other obstacle remained; remember when I said we *thought* our school had an APA-approved captive internship program? Around 1987, news circulated around our department that our internship program might not actually have that approval status. Seems our director didn't submit the paperwork on time and now had to beg the APA and play catch-up.

Since getting licensed in any state after we graduated required such status, this was a big deal. Feeling uncomfortable awaiting the outcome of that fiasco, most of us who planned to finish up that year decided to ensure that we had an APA internship by firing applications all across the country

Needless to say, this halted progress on my dissertation and put me through the ringer emotionally. With Pilar living in Columbus at the time, I wanted to ideally land an internship in that city. Because the only placement there resided at Ohio State University (OSU), and the competition seemed fierce, I had to apply elsewhere or stand a very good chance of not getting a placement at all.

Since we planned to relocate later on and live near my folks in New England, I also applied to a few internship sites in Connecticut and Massachusetts. After a series of interviews, both the internship site directors and the candidates started ranking their respective choices they must make on selection day—a day I'll always remember as "Black Wednesday."

The rules for this selection process say that neither the sites nor the candidates can tell the other where they stand in their ranking. This affects the sites because once they offer a spot to a student, they cannot offer it to anyone else unless that student rejects the offer. If the student says they'll "think about it," and awaits an offer from another program, the first site can watch all the other desirable candidates on their list disappear—only to have the student decline the offer at the day's end. To avoid this, directors either blatantly violate the don't-tell rule and ask students if they're the student's first choice, or they find other clever ways to get at the same information.

Students not wanting to find themselves without a placement when all is said and done must show equal deftness in finding out how high up on the internship site's list they are without asking this directly. As I would later find out, it simply does not pay to be candid through this maddening process.

On Black Wednesday, I held true to my aim of landing in Columbus the following year. I told two other placement directors who called me fishing for information on where they stood within my rankings that OSU topped my list. By day's end, I learned that all the OSU spots filled up and that I had fallen between the cracks.

Not only did I not succeed in getting placed in Columbus, I now found myself staring into a pit of despair about my professional future. Anxious, frustrated, and humiliated, I borrowed a car and drove to Columbus that night to tell Pilar the bad news in person.

Like many other times in my life, things eventually worked out for me. I successfully defended my dissertation in March of 1988, the APA *did* grant approval for my captive internship experience (all that pain and sweat for nothing, right?), and I landed a postdoctoral fellowship position in Connecticut just miles away from Pilar's new job and home.

I loaded up a borrowed car with my belongings on St. Patrick's Day, said my good-byes, and headed east to my family, my girlfriend, and my new life as a young PhD. Irish tunes crackled on the radio as I drove straight on through Pennsylvania's Pocono Mountains toward my homeland.

Chapter 11

The Homecoming

My return to Connecticut grew bittersweet shortly after my arrival. I expected the joy and relief typical of most homecomings. Unlike many families today, moving out of state for any reason marked a violation of company policy in my clan. A fugitive for seven years on the run in the Midwest, the time had come for me to resume my rightful place in the family hierarchy. A product of this ethos, I felt the strong urge to do just that. And in March of 1988, the lost son returned, and his family warmly welcomed him back into their fold.

My mother tells the story of how in the fall of 1981 she and my father came to Madison, Wisconsin, to help me get settled into my new school's surroundings. She recalls choking up as I turned and waved good-bye to them while walking out of their hotel lobby's doorway—all spruced up in my Frye boots and camel suede cowboy hat (yes, I fell prey to the fad sparked by Travolta's movie *Urban Cowboy*). Grinning with excitement over my new adventure—typical for me even now—I couldn't wait to discover what lies ahead of me. But Mom felt the loss inherent in all changes.

Mom was right to feel the loss of her oldest son. The ideal picture of my triumphant reunion seven years later clashed with the reality of my not being the same guy who left that Madison hotel in 1981. Most notably, the prodigal son returned with a girlfriend.

It probably would have been easier to slip back into my prior role and rejoin the family's daily life if I came back alone. But in fairness to Pilar—who had waited two years for me to complete school and had foregone the option of living near *her* family—I had to consider our need to reestablish a sense of connection after living apart for so long.

Yet the gravitational pull toward my family proved irresistible—and an inevitable loyalty conflict ensued during that first year in New England. I recall how everyone suffered. My family missed me and could not understand why Pilar and I could not simply live nearby and become a part of the Smith family system.

Pilar felt intimidated by the family's pressure to gather the flock for various and frequent events—baptisms, showers, weddings, birthdays, beach trips, basketball games, and golf outings—that seemed to occupy nearly every weekend. "When are we going to have time to get settled in our new town if we're always with your family?" she would ask.

What I know now is that much of the tension back then originated with my own inner conflict: my inclination to rejoin the family culture clashed with the independent spirit I had cultivated during my Midwest years. It was my decision, after all, to resist moving to the greater Hartford area. It was *my* idea, originally, at least, to settle in *Boston* with Pilar—farther still from the place I once called home.

But since Pilar came in as the newcomer, she took a bit of the blame initially for the strain in my family ties. I can vividly remember the pain of getting stuck in the middle of two powerful forces, which were seemingly vying for my allegiance.

No longer off at school, for the first time in my life I had to admit (more so to myself) that I now *chose* to live apart from my family. But back then, my family couldn't get that my not wanting to live too close had nothing to do with *them*. It was quite the contrary: their love and support of my personal development gave me an inner calm and resolve that I feel deep in the center of my soul.

I never meant to hurt them; I just wanted the best of both worlds—to walk a path less traveled and to be able to see my folks without having to get on a plane. Fair enough, but I'm ashamed that I didn't articulate that better then to avoid some of the finger-pointing at Pilar that took place.

Perhaps due to this rough undercurrent, things started to look pretty grim for my relationship with Pilar. It came to a head one cloudy afternoon when we got into a little argument outside her Fairfield apartment building. As I stormed across the parking lot to my truck, Pilar chased after me and said that if I left now, I shouldn't bother ever coming back!

The sting of her threat provoked an avalanche of pent-up feelings that we proceeded to unleash on each other right there in the lot. And we got loud. At one point, a driver passing by honked his horn, and without hesitation, we both spun around and flipped him off. Good thing it wasn't a cop.

We took it over to the side yard and continued spewing at each other. In my frustration, I heaved my key chain at a sign. Unfortunately, my support foot slipped on the wet grass, and I went down in the mud, sparking another wave of rage that rushed through my body. At least I hit the sign with my keys—or else they would have sailed into the woods to some hopelessly unknown hiding place.

Eventually, we ran out of steam and agreed to call a truce and to seek out a good couples' therapist. Ironically, when I went back to retrieve my keys later on, three of them had bent upon impact with the sign—the only three keys on the chain that I didn't own: Pilar's car and apartment keys—too scary.

Fortunately, cooler heads prevailed in the months that followed, and our brief couples' therapy helped us work through some important sticking points. My family and I also reached a better place in terms of our living in Fairfield County. As the picture of our relationship improved, we both shared our amazement that we could reclaim those positive feelings we once held toward each other. Perhaps more importantly, we felt that if this struggle could not break us up, we might actually have the skills to handle the challenges life throws at a marriage—and this set the tone for our decision to get engaged.

It's strange, but, in a sense, this same trial that nearly broke us apart became a cornerstone for the foundation of a deeply held trust still present with us today. It reminds me of something I once read about how trust grows: that you need to give someone the opportunity to hurt you in order to truly know if they are worthy of your trust—if they don't have a *chance* to break your heart, you'll never know for sure.

Pilar and I got married in April of 1990 in Old San Juan, Puerto Rico. This picturesque Spanish colonial town in her native island has a rich history spanning back over five centuries. Having mended our ties with my family, the Smiths came well represented to this special place, and I count our wedding day among the best experiences of my life.

During our engagement, I passed my licensing exam and became eligible to get paid by insurance companies for doing therapy. This opened the door for my starting my own private practice part-time. I planned to build my practice while still working for the state hospital and to eventually move to running my own show full-time (my father's son, I never thought I *wouldn't* work for myself one day—guess it's a family thing). But first, I had to find some affordable office space nearby.

Enter Dr. Bob Matefy. On a tip from our couples' therapist some months earlier, I heard good things about Bob. Once a University of Bridgeport professor, Bob had a well-established practice located on North Avenue, near the Fairfield line. A depressed industrial city on the Connecticut shoreline, the once-vibrant community of Bridgeport had fallen to hard economic times, and much of it had become a drug-infested eyesore. Located in one of the few remaining reputable parts of town, Bob maintained an office in a beautiful Victorian home.

From the moment I walked into his walnut-trimmed parlor, I felt at ease. His receptionist, Lorraine, greeted and escorted me through a spacious waiting room and offered coffee or tea. As I waited for Bob to finish with a client, I noticed his next client walked right into Lorraine's office area, smiled, said a friendly hello, and made her own cup of tea. Kind of like walking into a friend's house and feeling comfortable enough to serve yourself. I instantly liked the feel of being there, and I liked Bob—the architect of this warm office culture—even more. We hit it off quickly, and he offered me a place in his office to get my start in private practice.

Over the years since that fortuitous meeting—even after Pilar and I moved away to Boston—Bob has been an incredible mentor and friend. To this day, he remains one of those rare, bright affirming people I feel privileged to have encountered on my life's path.

Coincidentally, I had already found another positive connection located just down the street from Bob's office—one that had gently ushered me into the world of martial arts.

Chapter 12

My Martial Arts Roots

Summer 1988

    Master Ed Mezerewski looked up from his office desk when I walked unannounced into his tae kwon do school located on Wood Avenue in Bridgeport. Some of his students sat chatting on the floor of the *dojang* (school) stretching in their *dobuks* (traditional Korean uniforms)—their sneakers and shoes piled up in the foyer area I had just entered.
    I glanced back toward Master Mezerewski, feeling a bit awkward trying to figure out how to state my business. He just nodded, grinned, and got up to greet me. "How are you? My name's Eddie," he said pleasantly in a raspy voice as he extended his callused right hand to shake mine. Calcified from years of smashing it through boards, bricks, and God knows what else, his hand felt like a rough stone warmed by the sun.
    After a brief conversation concerning my interest in studying tae kwon do, the Master invited me to watch his next class, which was about to start. I have to admit that I felt a little intimidated by the idea of having him as an instructor; my first read was "Tough guy in a white uniform who could kick my ass from here to Sunday."
    In truth, I didn't know what to expect, but this person did not fit my image of the more serene martial arts instructor I had held in my head. I privately thought, *This ain't no Master Po (the omniscient mentor to the young character Quai Chang Cain in the movie* Kung Fu*), but what the hell? I'm already here.* So I stood and watched.
    What I saw captivated me. Taught by a Korean Grand Master, this instructor observed all the traditions of a formal dojang. His firm command of the class

seemed to come tempered with a certain tenderness he obviously held toward his students. Judging from his teaching style, I instantly knew Master Mezerewski could nurture my budding interest in becoming a martial artist. I came to class the next day as his newest adult student.

I recall bounding barefoot into the dojang with a mind wide open to the expansive possibilities the martial arts had to offer. The white belt that every neophyte student wears signifies a beginner's mind, unburdened and uncluttered with prior martial arts knowledge. Everything was new to me, and I had so much to learn.

A couple unpleasant surprises awaited me, though: like the importance of stretching your legs *before* you reach twenty-seven. And having calluses on the bottoms of your feet really helps too—a lot.

Several of my classmates—teenagers and adults who started stretching upon release from their mothers' wombs—could do 180-degree splits with their legs. These were *guys*. I had never seen a guy do a split before in person.

As for me, I could light a small campfire on the floor between my fully spread feet and still avoid severe burns to my groin area. But riding high on the enthusiasm of those early days, I saw rapid gains in flexibility. Between that and the sheer luck of having long legs, I could kick above everyone's head within the first twelve months.

My feet took quite awhile to recover from the assault to their delicate undersides. Since I never walked barefoot much, my feet literally had no calluses on them. And since students practiced shoeless on all-weather carpeting, I spent the first several months nursing rug-burns and the splits that formed in my nascent calluses. As my training continued, however, my feet toughened, and for the first time in my life, I could soon walk barefoot across a hot, pebbled parking lot. Even more surprising, I would later discover that my once-dainty size 14 feet could smash through three one-inch-thick wooden boards.

Still a relative newcomer to the Bridgeport area, I welcomed the companionship that emerged from some of the other adult students. We had all formed a good rapport and had fun catching up with each other before and after classes. Occasionally, we got together outside of class, and Master Mezerewski joined us periodically.

Consistent with my impressions of him that first day, our mentor turned out to be a genuinely good guy with a big heart and an easy laugh. He told us about how he got started in tae kwon do—how his Korean instructor, Grand Master Chae Rhee, took him under his wing at fourteen and later gave his student the honor of taking over his school when he moved to New York. He also shared his sadness with us when Grand Master Rhee—after an apparently strong disagreement over how his protégé should run the school—decided to end his long relationship with him.

One night, I witnessed perhaps the truest test of Master Mezerewski's character and of his commitment to martial living. It came after one of our fellow students decided to intervene in a clash between two neighborhood teenagers. It started across the street from our school, and the student went outside to break up the fight. After refusing to stop fighting, Master Mezerewski intervened and sat the teenagers down in his school waiting room until the police had arrived.

Later, around 2:00 AM, the police called Master Mezerewski at his home to inform him that his school had caught fire. When he arrived, the fire had already gutted his school building, destroying everything inside. You could always replace equipment and drywall; but he lost his trophies, photos, and other personal mementos. When me and some other students got there the next day, we could see our blackened school walls still smoldering—along with our Master's temper. We learned that one of the teens the police had picked up earlier from our school decided to pay our Master back by firebombing the building. They caught the kid but not before the damage had been done.

After some soul-searching and financial maneuvering, Master Mezerewski rebuilt the school with a little help from his friends and students, and the East Coast Academy of Tae Kwon Do still thrives now in that same location. What initially seemed like a spiteful teen's last laugh actually brought us all closer together as a group. In a way, we all needed to rally around this adversity, as if to say to that kid, "You're not gonna deny us our school."

Like most martial arts schools, Master Mezerewski had a written code of honor he expected us to follow in and out of the dojang. The last principle listed in his creed reminds you to "Never give up—persevere to finish what you start." Now, it's easy to have high standards, but the hard part comes when you get called upon to live up to them. In our Master's defiant refusal to succumb to his own devastating loss, he followed his own code and revealed to us the true essence of his character. Following his lead, everyone helped in various ways to rebuild the school, and that created an amazing esprit de corps in the new dojang.

Interestingly, another group to which I had belonged at that time had also gelled by the same process of rallying together around change—the gang I worked with at the hospital. The treatment units in which we worked faced extinction due to dwindling state funds. This meant streamlining and revamping a psychiatric delivery system that probably predated Eisenhower. Without making these changes, the hospital would have to lay people off and, in so doing, deny adequate care to many severely disabled patients.

In a visionary gesture, our administrators reasoned that if our staff got a chance to design our own patient treatment program, we might take more ownership in seeing that it would work. That's exactly what happened: we saved the Day Hospital program by building it together from the ground up. Team morale shot through the roof, and patients got better care.

These two examples demonstrated the power of giving people a chance to participate in developing something meaningful together. A barn burns down (or a dojang, in Master Mezerewski's case), and the townspeople band together to rebuild it. When you feel like you're making a significant contribution to something, you're going to want to see it succeed. I think it taps into our basic need to feel valued, empowered, and connected with others—and I've seen this same phenomenon occur in companies, teams, and families.

In 1991, Pilar and I made the decision to finally make the move to Boston. We knew our moving to Boston meant losing many good connections we had forged over the three years we lived in Connecticut—Bob, Master Mezerewski, and others. As for my martial arts training, at that time, I only had a short while to go before testing for my black belt in tae kwon do. By then, I had reached the second-degree brown belt level. Given the circumstances, Master Mezerewski generously offered to have me come back to his school so I could test for black. I fully intended to do this after getting settled in Boston, but it never happened. The mania of getting my practice started in the Boston area took over, and sadly, I never even saw my first martial arts instructor again until many years after we moved.

But the seeds he planted in me to continue pursuing martial arts had taken a firm hold. A few months after arriving in the Boston area, I began my search for a tae kwon do school so I could resume my training.

Chapter 13

Intro to Karate: Esposito Style

We found an affordable two-bedroom attic apartment in the Nonantum section of Newton, a small city located just west of Boston. Locals also call Nonantum "The Lake," because it sits on the dirt that city planners used to fill in the ill-fated Silver Lake to meet housing demands (copying Boston's idea of dumping soil from Natick into what we now know as the pricey "Back Bay" area).

Predominantly blue-collar in its origin, Nonantum has its own culture and dialect, with the many regions of Italy well represented among its citizenry. Because of its proximity to Boston, you can't touch a decent house in that area now for under $400,000, which probably reflects an appreciation rate of around 1,000 percent over the past thirty years. Not bad for the hard-working immigrant families who came here in search of the American dream a half century ago.

Driving down Adams Street one day, I saw a black sign posted outside a fitness center with gold faux-Japanese lettering that spelled K-a-r-a-t-e." Frustrated with not finding a reputable tae kwon do school nearby, I stopped in to learn more about this martial arts style. With a déjà vu-like feeling in my stomach, I walked into the place looking for another Master Mezerewski to train me. I turned left to shake the outstretched hand of a man who seemed to be waiting for me to arrive. He looked about two thirds my size, but that perception of him would soon change.

"My name's Joe Esposito," the guy said with a firm resolve. He wore gym clothes; and his thickly muscled hands, forearms, and upper body revealed his superb conditioning. While he smiled and laughed easily enough, I sensed in Joe an edge of intensity and restlessness. I knew right away that I had not found in him a Mezerewski surrogate. In fact, he did not even teach tae kwon do. But he seemed very knowledgeable about martial arts, and I kind of liked him, so I agreed to watch a class that Thursday at 7:00 PM.

I could affectionately call what I saw that evening "The Joe Esposito Show." This dojo was *his* stage, and from the moment he set foot on it, he became the master of ceremonies. "Okay, line it up," he said as he scanned the crowd while bolting to the front of the room. Another prospective student and I followed him. "Let's go five to a row; quickly now, we've got a lot to do tonight," Joe said before sitting us near him by the front. We faced the back wall mirrors and a class of around twenty-five students. They stood quietly at attention, lined up in perfect rows of five, awaiting his instruction.

From his first order, his students screamed their *kiai*s (the yelling you hear when students give and receive strikes) as they tried to keep pace with Joe. He walked quickly through the ranks while shouting out instructions. You could tell his mind worked at a rapid clip and that he expected you to follow his lead. But Joe seemed to insert just the right amount of humor into his teaching to temper his intensity with some fun. The room resonated with energy, and soon the mirrors got fogged over from the steaming bodies of his students.

When class ended, I found myself still staring, trying to process what I had seen. I looked over to the other guy who had sat next to me earlier, but he had left! He must have felt overwhelmed by the experience and thought this place was not for him. I never noticed him leaving. But Joe's energy and depth of martial arts knowledge impressed me, so I decided to give him and his kenpo style of karate a try.

As we discussed my decision later that evening, Joe asked me if I preferred to wear my brown belt in his class. I guess he wanted to acknowledge that I had prior martial arts training and was not a novice. But I preferred to enter his school as a white belt. I felt it best to let go of any ego associated with my rank at my former school and to assume once again that beginner's mind as I started to study a new fighting system. I never regretted that decision, as I would later appreciate how much I had not learned up to that point.

Joe began teaching me in 1992, and it would take me eight hard years to reach a stage in my development where Joe felt I was ready to take his infamous black belt test. This would come on the heels of many intense belt promotion tests that I had to pass to even warrant an invitation to the "promised land." In a later chapter, I will cover some of the details of those experiences that gave Joe confidence in my ability to rise to this challenge.

To understand Joe's style of teaching and living, you have to know his background. First, he is not a two-dimensional cartoon character. Like all of us, he is far from perfect and not always easy to understand. But whatever label you can pin on Joe, none fits more appropriately than the title *Warrior*. Everything he does in his life follows a certain logic, and beyond all physical training, his cultivation of the warrior mindset in his students sets him apart from most other masters.

Chapter 14

The Master

"You must train until near-death . . . then repeat."

Joseph Esposito, 10th Dan Black Belt

His father's namesake, Joe Esposito was born to fight. As a boxer in the navy, his grandfather would compete for the then-common purse of a gold watch. Joe admired his grandfather's substantial collection of golden timepieces. He recalls how he, his older brother Michael, his father, and his grandfather would play around with boxing drills at family events during his childhood.

Joe Sr. did not encourage his sons to fight, however. In fact, he wouldn't give them permission to join a local boys' boxing program. He feared his sons would get involved with some enterprising and seedy people in the boxing world who might impede their chances of becoming successful outside of the ring. Yet he could not suppress Joe Jr.'s interest in fighting. As Joe explains it, growing up a smaller guy in Nonantum, knowing how to fight came in handy. Beyond the practical need for self-defense among the local thugs, Joe idealized the heroes and icons of his childhood who knew how to brawl and answered to nobody.

At the age of twelve, Joe managed to persuade his father to allow him to enter a YMCA judo class—with the coaxing of a family friend who himself practiced that discipline, which originated in Japan. This reflected an even larger triumph for young Joe when considering the anti-Japanese sentiment still pervasive among World War II veterans and their families living in his neighborhood. In 1967, the consensus among them seemed to be that if we defeated the Japanese in the war, they had nothing they could teach us about fighting technique.

Joe's victorious entrance into the martial arts rather quickly turned into confusion and disappointment, however, as he got frustrated with his instructor's limited ability to speak English. Even worse, after spending hours grappling and throwing partners in the dojo, he realized he would never get a chance to throw one punch or kick in this style of fighting.

A wise guy and irrepressible spirit even then, Joe conspired to prove to his classmates that the techniques they had learned had no practical application in a real street fight. One day before class, he persuaded everyone to rush their unsuspecting and passive instructor. With everyone on board, Joe confidently led the charge against his teacher shortly after he entered the dojo. No doubt it would have been a glorious, if not chaotic, demonstration for all to see, except nobody else followed Joe into battle, and the instructor proceeded to mop up the floor with Joe's helpless body. "Let's just say that in today's legal climate, that instructor would never have gotten away with what he did to me that afternoon," Joe later chuckled.

Besides his insolence and undeserved cockiness at such a tender age, this story tells of a naïve but brave young man who sustained a one-man mutiny against a larger more skilled opponent. Joe must have realized his classmates' betrayal soon after he began his attack, but he kept on coming despite being thrown around the room. This set the tone for his later legendary exploits around the Boston area throughout his adolescence.

His father's concerns about Joe getting hurt while fighting notwithstanding, the genie was now out of the bottle. After his unceremonious departure from the YMCA judo program, Joe began a search for the more aggressive martial arts styles—those that included not only foot and hand strikes but also techniques in joint manipulation, pressure points, chokeholds, throws, and weapons.

Although he sampled many styles, Joe settled in on the versatility of kenpo karate, which encompassed a cross section of skills from many other disciplines. He earned his black belt by age twenty, and he went on to win many championship competitions in forms, breaking (boards, bricks, etc.), and fighting.

About a year after he earned his black belt, his teacher decided to return to service in the U.S. Air Force, which meant closing his school. This left Joe and his fellow students with the dilemma of where to train. Once again in his life, Joe chose the more risky path by starting his own school at only twenty-one years old in 1976.

The magnitude of this risk appeared even greater when considering that he had gotten accepted into the local police cadet program. As a to-be civil servant, Joe's decision to abandon his karate school to become a cop would have guaranteed his financial stability. His father—a man Joe considers as "the biggest influence in my life"—tried to reason with his son to think of his future. Nevertheless, he chose the path of teacher over policeman, and his school still thrives today.

With all the respect due to Joe Sr., the internationally known Grand Master Ed Parker perhaps holds a place as the biggest influence in Joe's karate life. At the very least, his close association with the person, whom people call the Father of American Kenpo Karate, certainly did wonders for Joe's credibility in the martial arts world. How they first met sprung from both Joe's complete commitment to his craft and from pure, unadulterated, dumb luck.

Apparently, while touring the local dojos in the Boston area, Parker happened to hear about a guy named Joe Esposito who drove a red Ferrari bearing the vanity plate, kenpo. Joe's name rang a bell for Parker, who had trained Elvis Presley. Coincidentally, he knew and liked a lively character of the same name who served as the King's road manager. Parker said he wanted to meet this guy (Boston's Joe). Upon meeting, Joe said they hit it off immediately, and from that point on, Joe offered to drive Parker to his many engagements whenever he came into town from his home base in California. Parker accepted, and they developed a strong rapport and mutual respect.

Joe tells of a story when he attended a clinic Master Parker hosted, where a man named Remy Presas—the grand master in arnis, a Filipino stick-fighting system—walked in unannounced with his best student. That his clinic would draw the attention of such a prestigious guest came as a compliment to Parker. But since you don't get to the position held by Parker and Presas without a fair amount of ego, this also put some pressure on Parker and his students to perform their best. Parker paired Joe off with Presas's top gun, and the contact during the ensuing drills and sparring started hard and got harder. As the intensity escalated, Joe clearly established himself as the more skilled fighter. Parker had to be pleased with his student's performance.

Afterward, Parker invited Joe to join him, Presas and his aforementioned student for dinner at a local Chinese restaurant. During the meal, Joe made the bold gesture of politely critiquing Presas's claim that one of his stick techniques could work interchangeably with knives. Joe asserted that performing the technique in question with blades instead of sticks would result in slashing the inner forearm (here we go again—recall the judo instructor whose skill Joe once questioned?).

According to Joe, Presas said nothing and just got up and left the restaurant. Joe said he could feel the burn of Parker's disapproving stare. Everyone sat there stunned, not knowing what to say or do. Shortly afterward, Presas returned with his sticks in his hand. He said that Joe was indeed right and then handed the sticks over to Joe as a gift acknowledging his perceptiveness.

Parker didn't say a word to Joe during the long ride back to his hotel. "It was an excruciating ride back," Joe said, "I tried talking about anything, but he just stared out the window." Finally, when they arrived in Boston, Parker turned to Joe and said he should not have confronted Presas in front of his student. Then the sternness of his glare softened and gave in to a conciliatory smile, and he added, "But that was great!"

Joe never had the chance to become Parker's top-ranked student. The last time he tested to move up another degree within his black belt, Parker told Joe that he was "Well under rank, but I can't double promote you to fifth degree." Joe asked him when he could test again with Parker, and he replied, "The next time I come into Boston." Grand Master Ed Parker died two weeks later of a heart attack.

Master Joe Esposito has complemented his long career as a martial artist with developing his skill in the use of various weapons. These include knives, bows, archery, rifles, and pistols. He has reached the master class level in action pistol shooting—used in the police training where you simulate actual scenarios cops face, which is requiring quickness, accuracy, agility, and the discipline to not shoot at friendly and civilian targets as they appear. He and his wife, Cathy (herself an amazing martial artist and now mother to two of Joe's three children), run Esposito's Karate Fitness Center in Newton, Massachusetts.

Only in his early fifties, Joe's boundless enthusiasm and his teachings have had a profound influence on the lives of many people. Besides civilians, he has trained prison guards, police officers, and marines in offensive and defensive techniques necessary to perform their jobs. His reputation in the martial arts world has landed him on TV shows, featured news articles, and a leadership role as past president of the Karate Referee's Association of New England.

Growing out of the cocky gunslinger days of his youth, Joe has walked the path of a responsible warrior with a code of ethics more appropriate for the samurai than the ronin. In the years I have known him since 1992, I have watched his growth as a teacher and as a person and am proud to have him as a friend.

Chapter 15

Martial Arts and Martial Living in Boston: Parallel Paths

In 1997, Pilar and I had our son, Evan. Like it was yesterday, I recall his grand entrance: no crying, just some soft whimpers, and lots of squinting with the brightness of the delivery room. And he looked like a caricature of his mother.

Evan's arrival filled us with the usual joy, fatigue, and dread commonly shared by most first-time parents. Having a baby can give birth to many fears. Some of my concerns included Evan's health, our financial picture, and my not having enough time with him. Stemming back to my hardscrabble days when I just started my practice in the Boston area—when I lost fifteen pounds and my life savings trying to build my business—I developed a Depression-era attitude about working crazy hours.

My warrior mindset and new contacts in the area eventually paid off, but it came at the price of limiting my time with Pilar and our friends. And I did not want to see that happen with Evan too. Even with my solid client base in 1997, managed care companies had forced me to accept lower rates to the point where I still felt compelled to work ridiculously long hours to earn a sustainable income.

So these feelings prompted my looking for ways to get off the fee-for-service, managed-care treadmill (insert mental picture here of George Jetson getting sucked into an out-of-control treadmill). I got on a search for more income *and* more time to be a dad. Before long, I found an at-home business opportunity that seemed to fit what I needed.

This opportunity came at the recommendation of a colleague I respected, who said he had found it profitable even working at it ten to fifteen hours per week. And since it involved building a critical mass of residual commissions, I could theoretically work hard at it the first couple of years and then coast a little while collecting the residuals. The concept of residual income reminded me of what my dad did over his entire career: he sold insurance policies, and with each annual renewal from his client base, he got a commission check. Because he and my siblings became good at selling—and I knew how to effectively sell my services as a psychologist—the prospect of selling a line of health products from a reputable company seemed okay.

After reviewing this idea exhaustively, I agreed to go for it. It started out fairly well, as I made some sales in the early going. A number of hitches became apparent rather quickly, which I chose to ignore at that time. Namely, while I am an expert in my specialty as a psychologist, I did not know a lot about nutrition, supplements, and the other health products offered through the parent company. Naturally, this made it hard to effectively answer questions raised by prospective customers and clearly affected my credibility and that of my product line. To address this issue, I tried to immerse myself in articles and audiotapes on my products, general nutrition, physiology, and sales and marketing strategies.

I also faced the challenge of having people trust the concepts of network marketing and direct sales. While people knew about and bought from companies like Avon cosmetics, Tupperware, and Dell computers, they seemed to wrinkle their nose when presented with the option of buying their vitamins from anywhere else but a retail store. For the first time in my professional life, people avoided my calls and at times got hostile with me. It became tougher and more anxiety provoking to pick up the phone.

"Welcome to the life of a salesman," I often mumbled to myself, "man, how did my dad *do* this for forty years?"

For me, perhaps the greatest sticking point of all, however, lay at the center of the network-marketing concept: you're supposed to approach people in your personal network, whom you believe might make a good customer or business partner. Except this violates a principle so obvious in my job as a psychologist—you avoid having multiple relationships (i.e., having friends, family, or coworkers as clients) with your clients, because this can hurt your primary relationship with them. Even outside of my profession, you may *not* want to have your nephew as your dentist—for example—because it's harder to complain about poor service.

In any case, I hung in there trying to make the business work, because I still felt things could turn around if I did. Remember Master Mezerewsky's honor code, which emphasized *never giving up*? Remember how that same attitude helped me become a college basketball player? How it helped Pilar and I stick together, and how I built my practice in a slow economy within a market already glutted with psychologists? Nope. My martial living code would not allow me to back down from the challenges I had encountered up to that point in this venture.

Meanwhile, a huge potential break for my psychology career emerged from my sport psychology connections. I had the chance to move my practice to a new $35 million sports complex called HealthPoint that would house the Boston Celtics training site and a state-of-the-art fitness center. The deal involved my sharing an office suite with ProSports Orthopedics and Physical Therapy, two thriving sports medicine businesses owned by the Celtics's team doctor and trainer, respectively. That the facility would sit four miles from my house had me giddy with excitement.

In November of 1998, I had alerted my colleagues and current clients at that time about my decision to move. HealthPoint would officially open its doors in April of 1999, and in the summer of that year, I transitioned my practice completely over to the new facility.

Although a bit slow at first, I could see the enormous potential to run a successful practice from this location. I even contemplated teaching karate there initially, as another income source and as a way to keep my techniques sharp for when I could attend classes at Joe's—which had become less and less frequent. But I was determined to not let karate slip away. Somehow, some way, I harbored the hope of one day testing for my black belt.

Chapter 16

The Invitation

The early spring of 2000 carried the usual promise of relief from another chilly New England winter. My practice at HealthPoint, by then a year old, had started to grow steadily. It had reached the point where I could not accept new clients needing evening appointments.

Funny how my heart used to leap with enthusiasm with every new referral. I recall my anxiety and frustrations with not getting any calls when I first started out. Now, I nearly began wincing when callers introduced themselves as someone looking to set up an appointment. The saying, "Be careful what you ask for," often came to mind. I've always strived to please the customer, and it bothered me when I had to disappoint someone who summoned the courage to reach out for help.

In contrast, my health products business continued to yield little return for the time investment required. By that point, I persisted out of sheer, stubborn pride and an obligation I felt to support the sales team I had assembled. Despite my growing awareness that this venture had failed, I still resisted the notion of quitting. Anything I had ever thrown myself into had achieved at least a modicum of success.

For a long time, I refused to accept that some Midwest farmer featured in *Network Marketing Magazine* could run circles around me in that industry. Pretty stupid reason to stay involved in a losing enterprise, I'll concede. This no longer reflected martial living but instead a refusal to admit I made a mistake taking on the project.

Besides my two businesses and my parenting responsibilities, I had also agreed to write a second edition of a book chapter on sport psychology, which I had originally coauthored with a colleague back in 1996. Given these commitments, it came as no surprise that karate had continued to take a backseat in my life.

But I never let myself go—far from it, in fact. While I never did start teaching that karate class at HealthPoint, I worked hard on my own to keep my techniques sharp. I continued to practice my kata, and I sparred with fellow students to maintain my timing and cardiovascular condition. Joe even went out of his way to meet me during the day to review upcoming test material. Nevertheless, I hadn't attended a class regularly in nearly a year, and I secretly worried that I might not ever get a chance to test for my black belt.

As if by intuition, Joe Esposito called me at my office on Monday morning, March 27, 2000. The tone of his voice told me he was up to something. "Hello Rawb!" he said with his unmistakable Boston accent, "we-ah running a black belt test with three of my oth-ah students, and I'd like you be the fourth; it st-ahts Monday, April 10th. Can you make it?"

While it sounded great, in my mind I thought, *No way*. But like a natural-born salesman, Joe proceeded to disassemble every one of my reservations about agreeing to show up on April 10. Previously, I had allowed myself to believe that too many obstacles had fixed themselves in my life to allow my making such a commitment. "You're not in that kind of shape," I'd said to myself, "and you don't have all your material; plus, who has the time to train for a grueling test that lasts sixteen weeks?"

Joe's black belt test had taken on a legendary reputation throughout the ranks on his school. This has happened for a number of reasons. Perhaps most prominently, like all tests, you don't get to see the questions or challenges ahead of time. Otherwise, people could prepare for everything in advance, and that would defeat part of the purpose of the test: to see how one responds to the element of surprise.

Another important reason is that Joe doesn't seem to mind fueling the rumors about his test. He *wants* you to take it very seriously. The standards he sets are very high, and nobody—not his close personal friends nor even his family (as his wife, Cathy, would concur)—gets a free ride. The motto you see on his school brochure reads, "Esposito's Academy of Self Defense: Where Rank is Earned, not Assumed."

Of the thousands of students who have trained under Joe over an impressive span of nearly twenty-five years, only twenty-four had previously passed his black belt test. This low number may conflict with the volume of black belts churned out by other martial arts schools, but Joe places strong emphasis on preserving the quality and meaning of this highest of ranks. This low number also adds to the uneasiness that plagues anyone taking the test over the entire sixteen-week period.

If the sheer length of time it takes to pass it doesn't intimidate you, then the rumors of how intense the training and pretests might. Students undergoing this test were often seen training and reviewing techniques and materials day and night. In classes, you could tell Joe targeted these students with his inquiries about techniques and martial theories. If Joe wanted to demonstrate some painful technique to the class, who did he pick as the uke (Japanese equivalent for practice dummy)? You guessed it, one of the students testing for their black belt.

During pretests, these students would all gather in the dojo after the last evening class, and Joe would close the door behind them. You could see the look of seriousness in their eyes and could only surmise what they faced behind the closed dojo door.

Despite all the hype and intimidation, the fact was that inside I had always wanted to test for my black belt. Up until then, I only had an honorary one, but that never sat too well with me—and Joe knew this. Ten minutes into my conversation with him, I began assembling in my head the various members of my support team that I would need to pull this off. In truth, just reorganizing my life around this test seemed as monumental a task as taking the damn thing. I hung up the phone and just stared up at the pewter-framed picture in my office of a lone fisherman surf casting off the rocks at sunset.

After a while, my mind drifted to a client with whom I've worked over the past few years. An adult child of an alcoholic parent, she has been taking care of people her entire life. Not surprisingly, she became a pediatrician, and she worked on a hospital intensive care unit for critically ill children. As a father of a young child myself, I'm continually amazed at how she and her colleagues can face the pain or death of helpless infants on a daily basis.

This client once confided in me a heart-wrenching story of how she had to help two first-time parents absorb the impending loss of their newborn to a fatal birth defect. Over an agonizing four-day period, she cried with these young parents, held their hands, and led them tenderly down the necessary path of accepting their unthinkable truth. Finally, the little girl's delicate life flame flickered out, and it was over.

My client's professionalism and compassion throughout this whole ordeal impressed me beyond words. I felt drained after hearing her story, and I've heard a lot of painful stories in my line of work. It was like I let this one slip through my protective emotional ozone layer. Most of the sadness I encounter in my practice hurts to an extent but more like a glancing blow that ricochets off into the cosmos. This felt more like a direct hit to my chest that stunned me. It made me appreciate more deeply my client's level of courage: she knows it's going to hurt, but she opens herself to it anyway—otherwise, she would be just another aloof doctor who refuses to make genuine contact with their patients.

But the most remarkable thing about this woman's extraordinary gift for her work is that she can't even go home to a peaceful place to decompress. At the time of this writing, her father has been dying of cancer, her own child struggles within the confines of a major mental illness, and her beloved husband—once her foundation of strength and support—suffers from an incapacitating neurological disease. Yet in the spirit of the pioneer woman, this young doctor must continue to circle the wagons and lead her family in the fight against all kinds of financial and emotional pressures.

As I thought of her and so many other resilient people with whom I have had the privilege of working, taking on the challenges of Joe's black belt test somehow seemed more doable. I was in. Now, I just had to tell that to my wife.

Pilar was surprisingly supportive when I spoke with her about it. Despite her utter disinterest in the martial arts, I guess she knew how important this journey was for me to undertake. One of the pleasures I enjoy in our marriage has been our supporting each other when we needed the freedom to grow personally or professionally. I appreciate this more when taking inventory of the many relationships where this does not happen.

Once I secured the commitment from my wife and several local baby sitters, I had only one component missing from my support team: the guys at ProSports sports medicine. Over the past year, a once-mild pain in my right shoulder had grown worse, and a magnetic resonance imaging (MRI) scan had revealed a full-torsion tear of my rotator cuff tendon. Many people my age with such injuries simply cut back on their activities and skip the surgery along with the six-month rehabilitation period that followed. But that would not fly with my lifestyle. So before Joe had even invited me to test, I had already begun considering the timing of my surgery.

I had consulted with Dr. Glen Ross, a young orthopedic surgeon working alongside my office in the ProSports suite. Trained at Duke Medical School and as a military doctor for several years, Glen had provided services for the navy athletic program in Maryland and now served as Dr. Arnold Scheller's protégé in working with the Boston Celtics.

Sitting there with my shirt off in Dr. Ross's office in early April, I asked him point-blank, "Glen, am I being stupid going through this test with my shoulder the way it is?" He simply smiled and said, "I didn't say that; in fact, it probably couldn't get much worse at this point. We'll just need to monitor you along the way." I wanted to hug him, but I just smiled back and thanked him for the encouraging news. My surgery would just have to wait until I completed the test in July. He then sent me across the hall to make a series of appointments with Woody to keep my shoulder intact over the next few months.

The man everyone calls Woody is actually Don Worden, a superb physical therapist who works alongside his partner, Celtics trainer Ed Lacerte. In his younger years, Woody traveled with the Boston Bruins hockey team as their trainer. Now forty, Woody works tirelessly at his craft in the ProSports office. A farmer, hunter, and fisherman in his spare time, Woody has that rare combination of superior skill and unparalleled bedside manner. Very down to earth, you feel at ease just talking with the guy. If my shoulder could go the distance, I knew Woody was going to play a key role.

With my team in place, I called Joe to have him save me a place on his roster. Now I had to smear on the war paint and get myself mentally ready for the test.

Chapter 17

The Test

The requirements for belt-rank tests across the many martial arts disciplines vary widely. Like any educational institution, martial arts schools differ often greatly in terms of the content and quality of their curricula. Schools can vary in their emphasis on the acquisition of crisp forms, self-defense or fighting techniques, the use of weapons, or personal growth.

You can usually tell their bent by looking around the premises to see what they display as their strong suit: do you see a balance of male to female students? If they flaunt the sparring trophies won by their students, doesn't this tell you something about their teaching philosophy? Do they have a solid program for kids? And how quickly can students progress through the ranks to black belt?

Despite my past experience with martial arts training, I did not expect the intensity and precision demanded during Joe's belt tests. He'll insist upon proper heel turns on kicks, the right snap in your punches—all the way down to knowing the four reasons why you sound out a kiai during a fight.

You can never overprepare yourself for one of Joe's tests. I thought I had done just that for my first test, hoping to show off to Joe how well I had adapted to his system. Unfortunately, while my techniques were sharp and my conditioning solid, I committed the now-obvious error of wearing an improper uniform to the event. Because of a backlog in my laundry load that week, I wore a dobuk (tae kwon do uniform) instead of a karate *gi* (Japanese for uniform). Never even gave it a thought as I stuffed it into my bag that evening. Nor did I ever have any reason to suspect that this could cause such a stir. I had worn it to many classes without so much as a peep of disapproval.

But this was a test, and as I was about to discover, Joe conducts his tests with the gravity and formality of a papal mass. Students must observe every custom at all times, and this includes wearing a *karate* uniform to a karate test.

Joe never dismissed me, nor did he mention his dissatisfaction with my dobuk. He didn't have to. Instead, three or four of his black belt assistants made it *their* business to remind me of my indiscretion all night long.

At one point later in the test, a group of us were allowed to rest while Joe queried some other students about some techniques. The catch to our so-called reprieve was that we had to squat—feet a shoulder and a half distance apart—facing a wall with our knees and toes touching the faux-wood-paneled surface. I couldn't tell which stung more: my rug-burned feet or the lactic acid buildup that caused my thighs to shake uncontrollably.

Nevertheless, I held my stance in my sweat-drenched dobuk—my mind switching between my body's cries of protest and a fantasy I developed about standing in the center of a refreshing mountain pool of water. My nose positioned only inches away from a knot in the paneling pattern, I stared deeply into it and drew deep, cool, soothing breaths. This served as an effective mental "happy place" for a while.

My reverie went undisturbed until a black belt suddenly whispered something in my ear, "If you think this is hard, we're not even halfway done (a total lie, but I had no way of knowing that at the time). Oh, and from now until Sensei calls you out, you'll have to keep this balanced on your nose." He then placed a dead fly on my nose—smack in the line of view of my mountain pool!

Surprisingly, this hardly fazed me. In a way, it seemed to have the opposite effect: that insect carcass further distracted me from the pain voltage crackling throughout my lower extremity. It also helped that I'd inherited my Irish uncle's flip at the end of his nose. This provided a suitable platform for my dead friend to rest peacefully.

That was the first and last test in which I had to endure any sophomoric hazing. It never bothered me, but that gag had more to do with flaunting power and had no place in a karate test—and today, I doubt Joe would ever condone or tolerate such meaningless antics. On the other hand, point taken: I always came to subsequent tests wearing my karate gi.

In later conversations with Joe, he told me that he designs his tests initially to implant in his students the basic building blocks on which all subsequent material would be built. He expects students at the earliest levels to memorize forms, techniques, and martial arts rules of thumb. In all tests, however, students must retain the skills they demonstrated in prior examinations.

Joe prides himself on his ability to shorten the karate learning curve. He says that over the years, he has figured out how to get students to acquire skills more quickly and to keep them motivated to learn more. Because of this, his low-ranking (newer) students tend to do very well at competitive tournaments—to the point where other martial arts instructors have often complimented Joe.

But Joe cautions that quicker isn't always better: a younger student can learn the techniques of a black belt and still not have a depth of understanding and mastery only attainable after years of training. As he puts it, "An eighteen-year-old race car driver may have better vision and reflexes but will lack the veteran's experience in handling all the situations that can come up out there on the track."

Joe's entire curriculum has undergone some important changes over the past decade. One area has involved his adding more frequent tests covering less material in each. I believe he does this for two reasons: first, given the choice of a superficial grasp of a lot of techniques versus a deeper understanding of less material, Joe would prefer the latter. Second, American students tend to need quicker, more tangible evidence of their progress.

Raised on sound bytes and thirty-second commercials, today's karate students seem to have a shorter attention span than their Asian predecessors (in fairness to these folks, they must contend with much more information than the pupils who underwent training decades ago). They simply don't have the patience to train indefinitely until their omniscient master deems them ready for promotion.

Another important change in Joe's approach to teaching karate involves his disposing of some of the forging tactics traditional to most martial arts. Part machismo, part practical combat for training, forging techniques were designed to harden the body and spirit to the pain and adversity that characterizes warfare.

These included activities like punching a wall or wooden post to repeatedly fracture the knuckles—allowing them to calcify and to deaden the skin covering this area, which enables the warrior to put their fist through wood, concrete, ice blocks, or someone's face without the pain such an impact would normally cause in your hand.

Similar forging can be done to other parts of the body (e.g., your shins), but they all literally cause permanent damage to that area. To avoid this, Joe replaced these types of training methods with greater athletic challenges to forge or toughen his students mentally and physically. "About the only thing I kept from the old system that isn't consistent with what we *know* is sound athletic training," he confides, "is that I still don't rehydrate my students during classes—which I know is a backward practice from the days where denying yourself water was supposed to show how tough you were; that'll come, but progress is slow."

Then there is Joe's infamous black belt test. This sixteen-week test of skill and will involves a commitment to teaching two and attending two classes per week. Joe's own sensei, world-renowned Grand Master Ed Parker, had actually required a third class taught and attended each week, and for years, Joe did too. Only recently did Joe modify his test to adapt to the realities of his clientele—who tended now to be older professionals with families, instead of younger students unencumbered by the same magnitude of commitments outside of karate.

As stated earlier in this book, Joe inserted four pretests designed both to demonstrate mastery of a variety of martial arts skills and to boost your conditioning level another notch. The rationale for this stepwise conditioning progression becomes abundantly clear when you consider the severe physical demands placed on you in the later stages of the test.

The first of these pretests involves a combination of distance and sprint training that initially can seem daunting. Because of all the running involved—in fact, there's not a trace of karate gleaned from this pretest—this event is often simply referred to as the Run. During the pretest, you have to run seven-plus miles within an unspecified time limit. After a brief water break, you must then do a 440—and 220-meter dash, followed by three one-hundred-meter sprints, and topped off by five sprints up a lengthy flight of stadium steps. If you're not much of a runner, this is a very painful initiation. But Joe likes to tell you (and he's right) that this is by far the easiest pretest.

With the exception of the Run, all other pretests take place at night. The only reason why the run starts earlier in the day is because the sheer length of time it takes to complete would carry us into the 2:00 to 3:00 AM range. The other pretests occur after Thursday-night classes (often Joe's most aerobically demanding of the week)—which we all had to attend as a warm-up for what we would face later on—thus the reason for the word "night" in the title of every subsequent pretest I'll describe.

The second pretest is called Kata Night. The Japanese word "kata" means "form" and refers to formal prearranged exercises practiced by martial artists for training purposes. Comprised of a series of offensive and defensive techniques and maneuvers, a kata represents a story to the trained observer. Each kata tells its own war tale in which the practitioner plays the protagonist engaging in combat with various imaginary opponents. Since practitioners use themselves as the height reference toward which they direct their punching and kicking targets, some say that every kata represents a battle with oneself.

Experienced martial artists can watch others performing kata and visualize the reenacted battle. By recognizing movement patterns, they can assess angles of attack from opponents, strikes blocked and thrown, and the likely number of combatants. Because of this, seasoned warriors can recall the entire kata after only one or two viewings—the same way we can retell a joke or anecdote we just heard.

As a competitor in tournaments back in the 70s, Joe won several championships in forms and weapons demonstrations. Accordingly, he always places a strong emphasis on acquiring the finer details of the many kata within his curriculum. Joe wants his students to master the art of storytelling through kata—complete with the requisite timing and dramatic flair. As you advance in rank, he works more closely with you on the subtle nuances of the kata—such as the crispness of a head turn, the eye focus on the next target, or how to make a smoother transition between moves—and how it links with other forms and specific techniques he teaches.

Like all stories, practitioners may interpret various parts of the form differently. Initially, instructors will give their take on what might be happening when you execute a certain move. By the brown and black belt levels, however, Joe expects you to develop your own interpretations of his forms and even to create your own kata. When he presses you about a rationale for certain movements within a kata, he no longer accepts answers like, "I don't know," or, "That's what Sensei Jones taught me."

Earlier on, you learn a large volume of material to memorize and practice. Later, you must deepen your knowledge of it and see how movements reappear in different ways across all your acquired techniques and kata. "I don't want a class full of well-trained parrots," he might say, reflecting on his aim of inculcating a depth of understanding martial concepts.

This idea reminds me of how the character Salieri in the movie *Amadeus* had served in the prestigious position of royal-court composer. His title implied that he was the finest in the land, since theoretically at least the king would only hire the best man for the job. Nobody knew better than Salieri himself, however, of his limitations as a musician and composer (he would later proclaim himself as the patron saint of mediocrity). In truth, he owed his high position more to his political savvy and arrogance than his musical genius.

When the brash, immensely talented young Wolfgang (Amadeus) Mozart started gaining a reputation for his musical brilliance—thereby representing a threat to Salieri's position and fragile self-respect—Salieri went to see him perform, hoping to see merely a well-trained parrot. Unfortunately, seeing Mozart play his own compositions, and so masterfully, revealed to Salieri the unbearable truth that Mozart's talent outshone his by far.

Where Salieri could write and play the notes, Mozart had a deep understanding of and connection with music. It just flowed out of him. This is what Joe looks for in his students: can they go beyond the recollection of movement sequences and flow with the ever-changing demands of their environment? That's when the mechanics become automatic and driven more by the warrior spirit. That's what Joe and any other instructor worth their salt looks for in their students at the black belt level.

During Kata Night, Joe assesses your depth of ability to understand and execute the advanced karate skills involved in all forms taught within his system. And since he does this virtually nonstop for three to four hours, this pretest doubles as another elaborate conditioning prelude to Hell Week.

The third pretest has earned the eerie title Bag Night. Naturally, the "bag" part refers to a variety of kicking and punching drills done on various bags and pads. Here you get to demonstrate your quickness, technique, power, and, of course, your stamina level. Unlike Kata Night—during which students can *never* speak to each other—a big part of Bag Night involves coaching and encouraging the partner you're assigned to for a given drill. Part of the evening's fun and games includes rotating round-robin style to different stations where you punch and or kick, and the partner holds the bag or pad and tries to keep you focused through your haze of exhaustion.

These drills only last two minutes each, but the rest intervals are kept brief, and the night goes on for hours. Boxers know all too well the pain you can sustain pounding away at someone continuously for two minutes, with precious few seconds to regroup between rounds. After a while, the guy holding for you can make or break your spirit. It really helps to have someone rooting for you to dig deep and let it all out. Unlike any other pretest, Bag Night is all about offensive skills, determination, teamwork, and comradeship.

The final pretest—Combinations, Punch Techniques, and Surprise Night (which I later refer to as technique night)—says what it does: it's a time to air out all you know about the twenty combinations and fifty-plus punch techniques that you learn along the road to your black belt test. It also includes your command of various defensive moves against clubs, knives, grabs, and holds.

The surprise part of that night involves some curve balls Joe throws at you to see how effectively you respond to the novelty of what he tells you to do. Examples might include having multiple attackers, performing techniques from different angles, or doing them in cramped spaces where you have to consider ahead of time which of the many techniques would make the most sense under the specific circumstances. The challenge here lies in keeping a cool head and trusting your body to know what to do at the right time. As soon as you start overthinking or worrying about botching moves, you're done.

Taking place just as you approach Hell Week, Joe tells you that this is the pretest, where most of his students that failed his test have stumbled. Perhaps this happens because of the surprise elements introduced or because of mental exhaustion. Or maybe students get psyched out because they have made it so far into the test that they couldn't bear the prospect of flunking so late in the game.

Assuming you make it through the four pretests, you advance on to Hell Week. Ideally, this should take place without all the outside distractions that life presents us with, but that almost never happens. People have families, school, work, and other factors that compete vigorously for their attention. This just adds to the drama of a superintense five-day period of training and demonstration.

The cumulative pressures of the entire sixteen-week journey gets packed into that week: you find yourself asking questions like, "What's he (Joe) gonna throw at us on day 1? Or day 2? Is my shoulder (or knee, back, elbow, or whatever ailment you picked up before our during the test) gonna hold up? How badly do you have to perform for Joe to flunk you at this point?"

The last week involves a testing session Monday through Thursday nights, each lasting three to four hours. Assuming you make it through the first four nights, you get a few precious hours of sleep before you have to come in and warm up for a 6:00 AM Friday session that lasts six to eight hours. Each night has a different area of focus, and Joe may spend more time on something he sees as less than satisfactory. By the end of the week, you will have to have adequately demonstrated a strong grasp of the martial techniques and theory, and that you can apply them under high levels of pressure and confusion.

Because he pushes everyone to the point of exhaustion—no matter what your conditioning level is—he watches to see how you respond under adverse conditions. This is how he attempts to construct the truest test of your martial expertise—the closest analogue to putting you in a life-threatening situation without actually risking your life.

A Final Note

In life, you must master the art of time management to achieve success. From my experience, formulating your plan—although essential—pales in importance compared to how you *execute* the plan. Anyone can *say* they want something. Getting it requires you to make literally hundreds of seemingly small choices daily, which reflect your *true* priorities and your ability to focus on them.

If you wanted to become an attorney, for example, but kept putting off studying for the law school admissions test, you'll likely blow the exam and fail in your goal. Instead of studying, habits like hitting the snooze button on your alarm, calling friends to chat, or watching TV eventually seal your fate.

I call such poor habits "bad mental hygiene," because they kill a plan like bacteria will overtake its host. Little by little, these habits and distractions suck the life out of your will to persist toward accomplishing your goal. In the pursuit of Joe's black belt, you cannot exaggerate the importance of managing your time effectively and staying on track.

Then there's the universal X factor in all realms of planning otherwise known as luck. Luck, whether bad or good, reminds us of the limits to the amount of order and predictability we can extract from an otherwise chaotic existence. Luck keeps us humble. It often drives us to perform random rituals and hold strange superstitions. Luck caused me to walk into a punch that forced me to withdraw from my first brown belt test four years earlier.

From a religious perspective, ancient Hebrew scholars warn that "Man plans, and God laughs"—certainly a sobering thought to control freaks spanning the millennia. But the alternative—to sit passively and wait for our inevitable futures—hardly seems preferable. Not to me, anyway.

So I humbly planned my life around a sixteen-week time block in pursuit of my goal: to earn my black belt. But life had taught me to travel hopefully while knowing that good and bad surprises would surely await me along the way.

Chapter 18

My Comrades

While karate seems like an individual sport, participants depend on each other in many important ways. They all train hard together and encourage each other. In the truest form of fair play and mutual respect, they acknowledge each other when someone executes a skill well—even when it was done on you.

When a student has had a clear opening in sparring, he or she pulls the strike just enough to avoid seriously hurting their partner (uke). Similarly, those practicing throwing skills refrain from dropping their ukes from the highest point in the technique, which could easily cause injury. They instead seek to break their fall at least somewhat as they crash down on the floor.

To maintain the honorable tradition of their art, senior students must observe and promote certain codes of conduct throughout the ranks.

The concept of fair play and teamwork applies even in tests, where people can pass or fail based primarily on their individual performances. For example, if you injure a fellow student during an exam to the point where they cannot continue participating in the test, Joe makes you bow out. This happened once to a highly skilled student on the last night of his ten-week brown belt test: he accidentally broke someone's nose. She got disqualified because she couldn't resume the test, and he failed outright for his lack of control. Likewise, if several students seem ill-prepared to meet Joe's test standards, he has often flunked the entire group and rescheduled their exam.

For Joe's black belt test, you cannot overstate the importance of working together with your fellow students. Consequently, if you had not grown close with fellow examinees over the years it took you all to even test for black, you will. You need that person to push you, critique your moves, and support you for sixteen weeks. You will have his or her cell phone number so you can schedule extra training sessions or to ask technical questions. You will spend more time with them than their families will—you will care about their personal lives. By the time Hell Week ends, you will develop a bond that will forever link you with a powerful (and empowering) experience.

Because of the key roles the three other students played in my black belt test experience, I want to say something about their backgrounds and motives for undertaking this journey. From an age perspective, we spread across a thirty-two-year span; the oldest was fifty while the youngest was only eighteen. While differing in leadership styles, personalities, and unique needs, we each shared a love of karate and a mutual trust in our collective intent to cross the finish line together.

My Comrades' Personal Backgrounds

I have to start with then-fifty year old Dave Coolidge, by far our senior member. With his youthful enthusiasm and dedication to karate, you would never guess that Dave would start receiving his social security checks in fifteen years. You would also never know how close he came to having a very different life path than the one he ultimately chose.

A native of New Haven, Connecticut, Dave grew up in a single-parent family. His father died when Dave was only five years old, and his mother raised him and his siblings alone. Always active—and sometimes at inopportune moments—Dave didn't fare well in school. Without a father figure to stabilize him, Dave got into partying early, and he dropped out of high school in the tenth grade.

He started out as a sheet metal mechanic but later became a carpenter. His wild days of youth eventually gave way to a wiser, healthier path, which included Dave's returning to school. Dave credits part of his turnaround to a World War II veteran who befriended him on the job. "He was a positive and encouraging guy, and he always helped me keep things in perspective," he recalls.

At twenty-seven, Dave received his high school graduate equivalency diploma (GED). By thirty-three, he had joined a men's hockey league, which he loved and only stopped briefly after he severely damaged his left hand in a table saw accident. Fortunately, his doctors saved his hand, but he spent the next year alternating between surgeries and rehabilitation appointments. Although forever grateful for the genius of his medical team, Dave never regained full use of the hand.

This did not keep him from playing hockey, however, as Dave returned to the ice wearing a special splint on his left hand. As the years rolled by, Dave's hard life as a carpenter took its toll on his back, knees, and shoulders. Consequently, he started to pursue night school to study architecture, and he now serves more in the design and planning of contracting projects.

At age forty-three, a friend convinced Dave to watch a karate class led by someone named Joe Esposito. Despite his declining physical mobility, Dave took his friend's suggestion in part because of his troubled past. He notes that "In my bar-hopping days, I got dragged into a lot of fights, and I got the crap knocked out of me many times . . . I always wished I knew more about how to defend myself."

He recalls getting blown away by what he saw one Thursday-night class at Esposito's school. Joe led the class in his usual intense way—everyone moving in unison to his sharp cadence—and Dave said he signed up for classes that very night.

From that moment on, Dave said he fell in love with the martial arts. "I worked very hard and had to deal with my broken down body," he confides, "but I never worried about pushing too hard for belt promotion—I just loved the journey, the discipline, overcoming personal limits. Plus, that was the first time in my life where I got a lot of individual coaching and encouragement . . . I missed all that when I dropped out of school as a kid."

Indeed, Dave has had to overcome a lot to pursue the study of the martial arts. But he does not complain, and he always greets his fellow students with a warm smile. One of those students, Dave's own daughter Sarah, completed the requirements for her junior black belt at the tender age of ten. On that subject, the usually humble Dave Coolidge doesn't even try to conceal his pride.

Dan Walsh grew up on the Lake at a time when every house had three or four kids living in them (Dan's house had five). "We must have had thirty kids my age on our street," he recalls, "we'd have street hockey or baseball games with other kids, our street against theirs." Always around sports, Dan learned how to compete and to deal with challenges. "I was a skinny kid, and people were always telling me I couldn't do things," he says smiling, "and I loved to prove them wrong."

One of those challenges included making his high school football team—which he did, of course—and this led to his taking his first karate class. A popular teammate of Dan's, Steve Nugent, had excelled in the martial arts and convinced his entire team to do their weight training at his karate school. Dan became interested in Joe's karate program and took his first class at Joe's dojo on March 17, 1983. His teammate, Steve, gave him private lessons in between group classes, and Dan got hooked on karate. From that moment, Dan told himself he would one day earn his black belt from Joe Esposito. "I didn't want to get my black belt from anyone else but Joe," Dan said, "and I've turned down job offers out of state so I could keep training at his school."

His plans for a black belt would have to wait, however, because after graduating high school in 1984, he joined the marines. Dan's uncles served in the marines during the Korean War, and as a kid, he recalls setting that goal for himself too. He remembers his boot camp experience at Paris Island and how well his sports and karate training prepared him for this infamous test of skill and determination. After Dan's term with the marines ended, he returned to Boston to attend college and resume his karate training. After college, Dan took the civil service exam to become a police officer, and he has served in that capacity ever since.

While Dan tends to remain private about his personal life, he keeps his karate background even more so. "In high school, some kids knew because our football team trained together at Joe's," Dan says, "and I remember a few times having friends say to other kids that I knew karate and could kick their ass. That bothered me a lot because I don't like being the center of attention in any way but especially not *that* way."

Dan guarded the privacy of his martial arts training so well that he never even told close friends or girlfriends. He would make excuses for why he could not go out with them on class nights and why he had certain bruises he sustained in training. "I had dated my wife for three years before I *had* to tell her," he confided, "she was my fiancé, and when I agreed to take the black belt test, I knew that with the time commitment involved, there was no way I could keep her from finding out anyway."

He progressed slowly and steadily through the belt ranks, with one notable setback that carried with it an important lesson. It came during the brown belt strength test, where Dan had underestimated the challenge of one of the events. He relied upon his athleticism to get himself through it, but he fell short even after Joe gave him a second try later that night. "I flunked that test because I wasn't prepared, and I didn't deserve to pass no matter how close I was," Dan acknowledged, "it was like Paris Island, where if you didn't satisfy the requirements, you got 'recycled' through the next platoon taking that test. They wanted you to pass, but you had to earn it. I believe Joe feels the same way about his students and his program."

Normally soft-spoken, Dan doesn't mince words when it comes to merit-only-based promotions in karate and in life. He feels strongly that letting someone slide by any test in life defeats the purpose of setting high standards and renders the significance of that test meaningless. On these terms, he accepted Joe's invitation to take the black belt test.

And finally, there remained the youngest—and perhaps brightest—of our bunch: Steven Leckie. We all knew his dad, Dr. Rob Leckie, from the years of having him as a black belt instructor at our dojo. Originally from Canada, Steven's father grew up with a steady diet of hockey. In fact, he played varsity hockey for Harvard as an undergrad before he attended medical school back in his native country. Besides his high level of karate knowledge, Rob holds a reputation as one of the top anesthesiologists in the Boston area.

Steven was born in Ottawa while Rob finished med school. He and his parents moved to Boston when his dad got a residency appointment at the Beth

Israel Hospital downtown. Sadly, his parents divorced when he was three, shortly after the birth of his younger brother, Jake. Like most children of divorce, the division of the family deeply affected Steven—yet he managed to maintain the near-impossible balance of staying connected to both parents.

Both of his parents remarried within a few years after their split, and Steven bonded well with his new stepparents. Shuttling back and forth between his parents' homes, Steven excelled in academics and art, and he played the clarinet in his school band. Like his father, he also loved playing hockey. And, despite his mother's misgivings, at thirteen, Steven attended his first karate class.

Steven admits now that he didn't like karate at first. "I seemed to do everything wrong," he now says laughing, "but I stuck with it. I found that it was a great way for me to connect with my father. I was always pressing him to teach me a new technique or form, and we would do boxing drills together at home."

Given Rob's stature at the dojo, Steven also enjoyed the extra attention showered on him by his dad's fellow black belt friends. "They would always push me a little harder and showed me cool stuff outside of class," Steven says.

Around a year and a half after Steven began to learn about karate, he had what he calls the most influential experience of my life: the loss of his baby half brother, Connor, who died unexpectedly of meningitis. "It was the only time I saw my father cry," he recalls sadly, "and then shortly afterward my dad and step-mother got a divorce; so right after I picked myself up from Connor's death, I got knocked down again."

Perhaps owing to his resilient lineage as much as his karate training, Steven did pop back up again. So did his dad. When Steven was sixteen, Rob married his third wife, Annette, another highly skilled black belt from the dojo known for her picture-perfect techniques. Their collective enthusiasm for martial arts further stoked Steven's interest in "Soaking up as much knowledge and technique as I could," as he once stated.

Always the consummate student, Steven cruised through the ranks in karate while excelling as a scholar athlete in high school. Despite his ravenous appetite for training in karate, almost none of his classmates at Brookline High School knew about his martial skills. "I never got into fights, and I never discussed kenpo outside the dojo," he says almost coyly, "I'd just disappear for a few hours to train and then reappear again, like Bruce Wayne as Batman."

Like Dan Walsh, Steven prefers to keep his karate expertise private. His father, Rob, concurs, "If you wear that stuff on your sleeve, it makes you look bigheaded and maybe even putting out a challenge to the world to take you on." He points to the historical precedent in Japan and elsewhere of keeping your martial arts training secret because it was illegal. "The student would slip away after working a full day in the fields to his teacher's house and train," Rob notes, "then he would sneak back home under the cover of darkness and not make his training known to anyone." These men feel that keeping your ego out of karate lets you focus more on training than on whatever admiration it may afford you from others.

Shortly after getting an acceptance letter from Harvard University as a premed student in the fall of his senior year, Steven received another important piece of news: Joe had deemed him ready to test for his black belt that spring. Given Joe's stringent standards in this matter, Steven's opportunity to test for black after only four years in the dojo reflected an accomplishment that may have eclipsed getting into Harvard. But as noted earlier, taking Joe's test and passing it were two very different matters.

With only a few weeks to go before the test would begin, my comrades and I prepared ourselves to take on our first big hurdle: the Run.

Chapter 19

The Long Run

Monday, April 10, 2000, was the official starting date of the black belt test. If a journey of a thousand miles begins with a single step, I virtually tripped out of the gate. Because of the sheer length of this exam, I expected to have something in my personal life conflict with some aspect of the test schedule. In such cases, I figured I could just maneuver my own itinerary to make it all fit together nicely.

This held true except in the case of my tenth wedding anniversary: that date could *not* be moved. Pilar and I had previously booked a week in the Virgin Islands to celebrate, and we had already paid a hefty deposit. Our trip unfortunately conflicted with the date of our first of four pretests. And yet, quite simply, if I wanted to see year number 11 with my wife, I was *going* on that trip, test or no test.

So right off the bat, I found myself lobbying for a change in our first pretest date to a mutually agreeable alternative. Joe made it very clear that it was my responsibility to coordinate this change to fit everyone *else's* calendar. A few phone calls back and forth with my fellow examinees, and I confirmed a new date: April 26. Lucky for me, Dave's wife—after hearing that my tenth anniversary plans hinged upon moving the pretest date—made the schedule change possible by graciously rearranging her work hours. After thanking her profusely, she said only half jokingly, "It was for Pilar."

"Whew," I said to Joe on the phone as I shared with him the good news.

That's when Joe questioned whether I confirmed that the local high school outdoor-track facility he uses for this pretest would be available on that specific afternoon. A track practice or home meet that day would eliminate our chances of holding our pretest there. Sure enough, when I called the school, they had a meet scheduled on the twenty-sixth. Getting scared that I might not find a suitable alternative date, I started my next phone conversation with Joe by just blurting out, "Shit!"

Joe reassured me that we could still do the run that day as long as I could find other accommodations for us. We only needed a facility that had a track and some stadium steps—except we had to find a place that allowed someone to use a bicycle on the track. That's because Dave needed to ride his bike for the distance-run portion of the evening. The guy's in great shape for fifty, but he's got ninety-year-old knees—and he'd never be able to make it to work the next day, maybe even the next week if he tried to run it. Joe worked around this issue by calculating the cycling equivalent to the energy expenditure involved in running seven plus miles (this meant Dave would have to start much earlier than us, like two hours earlier). Unfortunately for my dilemma, this accommodation already excluded two local school facilities, as they feared the damage Dave's bike might cause to their track's surface.

Then I recalled an asphalt course I had jogged on at a nearby college campus. Through a connection I had in their athletic office, I spoke with their director. He mentioned that the school's track team—which had sported several national champions—no longer used this venue and trained indoors. He had no problem with our using his outdoor facilities, but he warned that it hadn't been resurfaced in years. Of course, I didn't care about this, so to ensure that we wouldn't be overly imposing, I asked specifically if we could ride a bike on the track. "Hey," he quipped, "if you promise not to run anyone over, you can drive a car on it."

With a sense of relief, I called Joe. "Looks like it's a go," I said in a triumphant tone. "That's great," he responded. Then he inquired about the stadium steps, "I may be wrong, but I don't think they have any steps to speak of. How are we gonna run that part of the pretest when all they have is a small set of bleachers?"

My heart sunk again. "How many steps do we need?"

"More than they have," Joe said, careful not to reveal more about the test than I should know.

Back to square 1.

Joe then interrupted my emerging despair with a compromise, "Okay, we'll do all the track events there, and then we'll drive quickly over to Newton North to run their stadium."

I humbly but readily accepted his generous offer and shared the news with my comrades so that we could make our respective plans. The Run was on for the twenty-sixth.

With the first pretest just two weeks away, I had to stack up my schedule of classes to make up some of the lost time I would sustain after going away for my anniversary trip. The same would have to happen upon my return. My schedule comprised of my teaching the kids' and low-rank adult classes, followed by my attending my own class to refine my techniques. This all came at a time when my practice had bulged out of the sides of my already insane calendar. Oh yeah, then in my spare time, I had to log seven or eight miles of road work, three times per week to prep for the Run.

As for Evan, my list of babysitters at that time ran three-deep for any possible contingency: I had to leave room for their own agendas to clash occasionally with mine. Someone had to have an unexpected accident, homework assignment or hot date—and I absolutely could *not* be caught unprepared.

On days where Pilar could cover me, I would literally arrive at the gym minutes before a class; having already worked out, she would await the "hand off" of Evan (not even three at the time) in the lobby area. People would stare or shake their heads in disbelief, and we could only smile and nod along with them at the absurdity.

Surprisingly enough, my training and schedule went along as planned, and I felt fairly ready for the first pretest. At least as ready as one could feel walking into a dark room with all the furniture newly rearranged.

As the twenty-sixth approached, I had to simultaneously prep for my pretest and pack my bags for eight days of fun in the sun. The contrast of busting my ass for a severe physical feat while getting ready to lounge around for a week of pink drinks and calypso music seems comical even to this day.

On Wednesday, the twenty-sixth, my eyes jerked open at 5:30 AM. *Shit*, I thought to myself as I squinted to read the red neon numbers showing on my clock. Fifteen minutes before my alarm would begin its daily ritual of awakening me to the sound of classical music (somehow, Mozart's sweet melodies seem more merciful than the startling shrill of most alarms).

It didn't matter that morning. There was no way I could drift back to sleep, regardless of how many times I hit the snooze. My mind had already sounded its own alarm in anticipation of the Run. While my bags were nearly packed for Friday's trip, I had some important business to finish first.

I tried to quiet my racing thoughts as I staggered down the hallway toward the bathroom. "Don't rev up too soon," I reminded myself, "you've got a long way ahead of you before you get to the track."

As any competitive athlete knows, those preperformance jitters come with the territory on game day. They signal your body to prepare itself for a strenuous experience of uncertain outcome—and it's that very *lack* of certainty that gets your juices going. These feelings had grown familiar to me, ever since I began my athletic career as a kid. It took me years to discover that this nervousness is normal—and in fact provides you the necessary energy to do your best—and not necessarily predictive of imminent doom nor a sign of personal weakness.

The key lies in effectively channeling and capturing this power source and then drawing from this stored reserve as needed during the performance event. The art of timing when to rev up and when to cool your jets down usually comes with having experienced disappointing performances, namely, when you got too hyper and lost your composure or when you came out flat and never got the intensity you needed to do well.

I had to wear an overcoat to work that morning, and the weatherman said it might not crack the forty-degree mark all day. Making matters worse, his forecast included, "Periods of rain and wet snow". "That's just great," I said aloud to myself in the car. I went into the office late that day after dropping my son off at his preschool, and I had six clients to see before I headed out to the track. *A light workday for me*, I thought.

All day long, I couldn't shake the little voice in my head reminding me of the big event scheduled for later that afternoon. I honestly believe I held sufficient focus to help my clients that day, but that voice periodically fought for my attention. After my last meeting, I changed, grabbed my gear, and rushed out to my car. Unfortunately, the weatherman got it right that day: a chilled, windy, spitting rain dropped from a darkened sky. "Hey, at least it's not snowing," I told myself sarcastically.

When I arrived at the track, I quickly spotted my comrade Dave biking it around the loop. Annette Leckie could see Dave spinning around the track from the comfort of her nearby office window. Joe and a few other black belts sat watching in the bleachers donning ponchos and umbrellas.

Already completely soaked, Dave waved and chuckled as he sped by us while we did our best to loosen up. We returned the light-hearted greeting, both as a show of moral support and to acknowledge the ridiculousness of doing this under such poor weather conditions. Then we returned our focus to Joe, as he reviewed with us the rules of the first event that day.

The Run would last for twenty-eight counterclockwise laps around the quarter-mile track. It would begin with all of us quickly falling into a single file in the first or innermost lane. As we finished each lap, we would switch as a group to the next lane and would do so until we completed the outermost lap—at which point, we would start again on the inside lane. This system would allow both the witnesses and the participants to better keep track of our progress.

We would each take a turn in the lead position, which we would maintain for one mile, and we could decide in advance the order of assignment for that role. Joe then finally told us the time limit within which we had to complete this run (which, of course, I need to keep confidential for future students taking this test).

Looking back, I wish we didn't let Steven start off as our pacesetter. A cross-country runner in high school, Steven was the youngest and by far the strongest runner on the track. He got us off to a quick rhythm, and I found myself breathing hard earlier than I had expected in the run. Dan, a former U.S. Marine in his early thirties, kept a slightly slower but still crisp pace.

Halfway during Dan's first shift, I started to feel a stitch growing in the left side of my abdomen. Not good news. Any distance runner will tell you that these cramps tend to get worse, not better, and I still had five and a half miles to go—never mind the other festivities. This disheartening development could only be topped by the next change in my game plan: the rain turned to intermittent sleet and wet snow. Damn that weatherman.

I calmed myself and focused on proper breathing technique to avoid making the cramp worse. When it came my turn to lead, I slowed us down and recovered somewhat, although the stitch would continue to plague me the rest of that evening. The guys nudged me a little to pick things up, but I told them I needed to regroup, or I might not make it. They seemed to accept this, but it didn't stop them from pushing the envelope—mine probably more than theirs—when they took the lead spot.

My internal distress must have showed on my face, at least somewhat, because at one point late in the run, Joe asked me if I was okay. By then, I felt a mixture of fatigue and frustration, and I recall replying, "I'll make it even if I have to f—ing crawl." It must have come across as bravado, but by that stage, I somehow knew that nothing short of a massive coronary attack would prevent me from finishing.

Steven took full control of the run by the last two laps, and he finished a half lap ahead of me and a hundred meters or so in front of Dan. Dave had also finished his marathon ride (logging a quick two hours, forty-six minutes time). True to the team spirit of the event, they all cheered me on as I gratefully crossed the line. Despite the foul weather and my cramp, we all completed this first event with plenty of the allotted time to spare.

Next came the 440 sprint—roughly one lap around the track—followed by the 220, half a lap, then three 100-meter sprints, and finally, five sprints up the stadium steps. Joe let us catch our breath between heats, but this meant nothing if you had no depth in your conditioning level, that is, when you train for speed and endurance events like this one, it's not enough to pull off a good time in a single straightaway sprint. This event gives Joe a look at how many times in a row we could do it before falling apart.

By the end of the evening, I felt a significant lapse between the desire in my head to haul ass and my legs' response to my commands. They got rubbery by the last one-hundred-meter sprint and very wobbly later going up the steps. Nevertheless, we all made it intact and very relieved. Joe and his witnesses complimented us on making it through this pretest and dismissed us into the now-abandoned and darkened parking lot.

On the way back to our cars, Dave confided that he arrived at the stadium steps later than us because as we drove over from the track, he couldn't start his car. Apparently, Joe saw him sitting in his car looking downward and walked over to ask him what happened. When he got to Dave, Joe noticed that he seemed to have no control over his hands. He explained to Joe that his fingers got so cold during his nearly three-hour ride in the rain and snow, he couldn't move them. "It's okay," he told Joe, "I got the keys in the ignition now, and if I can just turn them to get the car started and get the heat going, I'll be fine." Joe shook his head and reached in to turn on the ignition. We all had a good laugh and got into our cars.

As I wearily but happily drove toward my house, I had to make an emergency pullover. My legs voiced their final call of rebellion for what I had just put them through—both thighs knotted up with cramps. Fortunately, I soothed them on the roadside and gently stretched them back into place for the ride home.

Time now to wrap things up for my anniversary trip to St. John's.

Chapter 20

Kata Night

We left for St. John's in a blur of exhaustion and excitement. Like so many people, vacations cause a rush of added work to clear your affairs before you leave—only to return to a new pile of stuff to do. That's why it makes sense to allow yourself a couple days' vacation before you actually set foot into your office. It kind of eases the transition back from island mode to whatever speed your life is like at home.[3]

The dry, hot air of the St. Thomas airport hit us as soon as we walked off the plane. The sun beat down on the palm trees and runway asphalt; but Pilar, her sister, our brother-in-law (they came to celebrate their tenth anniversary too), and I couldn't have cared less. By that point in our trip, we only had to grab a cab to the St. John's ferry and kick back at our guesthouse for the next week. On cue, the steel-drum calypso music played inside the terminal as we claimed our bags and scored some duty-free booze.

We had only seen the place we planned to stay that week over the Internet, but those grainy pictures never did it the justice it deserved. Designed and built by a successful local artist—filled with his ceramic works, of course—this

---

[3] Not that it's all bliss even if you live on a Caribbean island, as we found out during our stay in St. John's. While there, we picked up a book written by a woman who moved from the United States after falling in love with the island's charm, beauty, and laid-back lifestyle. She described some of the difficulties experienced by people similarly drawn to living in the islands. I guess the combination of a dramatic lifestyle change, and the various degrees of disillusionment in finding meaningful work had driven many of them to become depressed alcoholics.

gorgeous house sat right smack on Rendezvous Bay. We had our own little beach and awoke every morning to the sound of pelicans and sail lines gently tapping on moored sailboats.

For me, every day started off with a power run up and down the steep, jutting hills that make up much of this volcanic island. Before or since that trip, I never found it easier to take on St. John's unforgiving slopes. You would think I'd had enough of running for a while, and I did, but I had few alternative ways to keep pushing my cardiovascular level. So I would put on the pot of coffee before lacing up my sneakers and would return after my run to a cooling plunge into the bay. Sipping a cup on the shaded stone terrace afterward, I would read until everyone groggily made it downstairs.

Another way I kept up my conditioning involved practicing kata. Besides rehearsing these forms in my head while running, I would find a flat open area and do them continuously end to end. This helped to keep fresh in my mind the various nuances of each of the thirteen different katas I learned over the years. On Kata Night, Joe would expect us to know them all backward and forward, literally.

Having tripped me up with this material fairly easily during a prior brown belt test, I *knew* I needed to prepare for any of Joe's questions or drills. Joe loves to develop new ways to assess his students' comprehension of how the forms and techniques intertwine within the kenpo system.

An old favorite of his, however, called Stop Kata, involves his stopping you midway through a form. Frozen like a statue, Joe tells you to do things like, "Okay, go to another form that has the stance (or block, strike, etc.) you're in right now and complete that form. Go!" He doesn't give you time to think before he says go, either. You're supposed to have it flash into your mind, and then you flow into the next form.

This mimics the learning of a new language—first, you have to translate everything from English to Spanish, say, and then you get to the point where the words come to you directly in Spanish. Then you become fluent. In the same way, Joe expects you to become fully fluent in his system by the time you test for black.

As I did during my brown belt test, most people get mentally locked up over his pressure tactic. If you have not become fluent in the kenpo system, it takes you longer to process his directives. Then, if you add the worry of Joe's possibly flunking you into the mix, it bogs down the system and you stand there frozen with a blank look on your face. Not a fun experience. Not when you get that close to earning your black belt. No way in hell did I plan to let that happen to me on Kata Night—or any other night, for that matter.

Pilar, Maria, Randy, and I—a group that has always traveled well together—had a spectacular week. After spending our days at some sandy white beach, we made fabulous dinners at our house on the bay, listened to tunes, and toasted each other every evening for our tenth anniversaries while the sun dropped into the sea.

I went crazy with my video camera that week, and I recall having Randy film me our last morning while I fed hibiscus flowers to a large but friendly iguana. To avoid spooking him away, I crept slowly on all fours toward his rocky, sun-baked perch with the crimson flower in my mouth. Seeing the replay of myself on camera struck me at how taut my body appeared. Even after a hedonistic week, my body-fat count probably hovered around ten percent—roughly equivalent to that lizard snapping the hibiscus away from my outstretched hand! Hmm, efficient, powerful, and quick as an iguana—I didn't mind the metaphor and hoped I could carry those same qualities back with me to the dojo.

We returned to Boston on Sunday, May 7, and I jumped right back into my work and karate schedule. I know what I said earlier—that you should leave a day or two to transition back from island mode—but I didn't say I always followed that advice. Besides, I had fallen way off the test pace and needed to catch up.

The following Saturday, the guys and I met for three hours to practice continuous kata and critique each other's form. Besides serving as a conditioning drill, stringing all our forms together in the same order helped us in at least two other ways. For one thing, we had to match each other's tempo—which Joe would expect us to do on Kata Night—and secondly, we could detect errors any of us made in the angles we took when turning. If even one of us turned a few degrees differently from the rest, it became obvious because we would start bumping into each other.

Our first session practicing this together that Saturday looked like a fool's fire drill. We went all over the place. Enlightened by our observations of how poorly we performed as a group that day, we agreed to meet more often together outside of class.

Dan struggled with his knee, which blew up after the Run. This represented a potential disaster for his continuing the test, because he couldn't bend his knee past the halfway mark. An orthopedic doc reassured him, though, that he just strained it and that the swelling would go away with ice and anti-inflammatory medication. So Dan elevated the knee after workouts and popped anti-inflammatories like M&M's for a couple weeks.

Meanwhile, my practice seemed to withstand my absence. New referrals came in to replace the hours in my schedule vacated by clients ending their work with me. A pro athlete with whom I liked working called me back to come in for a mental tune-up, and I started a stress management gig with some local companies.

These assignments marked a refreshing change from the almost exclusively clinical practice I had in prior locations. The HealthPoint scene started to attract for me a generally healthier, more motivated kind of client—which often translates into their doing better in therapy. It also pays the bills, because they usually have jobs and, more importantly, health insurance.

Private practitioners like me typically have a love-hate relationship with insurance companies. Since most people prefer to use their insurance instead of paying out of pocket, the vast majority of my income draws from these third-party payors. But as I said earlier, the dominance of managed care programs forces me to spend unpaid time writing frequent reports, playing phone tag with insurers, refiling claims, and jumping through any number of other hoops just to get paid for my services—which I've already provided, by the way. I can't recall my services the way banks can repossess your car if you balk on a loan. Although at my lowest moments, I've fantasized about driving a few insurance adjusters crazy out of spite.

And with clients, you can't just stop therapy with them if they refuse to pay a bill. In my profession, if a miffed client utters the word "abandonment" to a state licensing board, it's time to call your lawyer. I used to take deadbeat clients to small claims court, with reasonable success. But these days, at least, I find it's better to eat the bill and gently extricate yourself from your work with such people.

Then there's the folks that pay up front and out of pocket. They often do this because they don't have a clinical diagnosis and can't use insurance, or they prefer to guarantee their privacy—in effect, nobody can find out that they're in therapy if there's no paper trail.

The prospect of a full caseload of such clients gives many clinicians a warm tingling sensation, because it sidesteps all the hassles associated with filing claims. And it dramatically improves the cash flow of their business. I have found that these folks come few and far between, because even some of the wealthiest clients I see prefer to use insurance if they can and often grumble when their copayment increases five dollars.

Thursday, June 1, Kata Night

The last three pretests before Hell Week take place on Thursday nights. Remember Thursday-night classes? That weekly cardio blowout session that freaked out the other guy who came to watch that first night I went to Esposito's? Well, Joe likes examinees to take this class before the pretest just so he can warm you up for what comes afterward. It's also a chance for him to more closely scrutinize your techniques. While doing this, he tends to get tougher on you when you're not up to par.

That night, Joe had us do our most advanced forms, and I felt unusually on that night. Perhaps that served as a good omen. After class ended, we headed down to the locker room to change into a dry gi. As we hopped back upstairs to stretch out again in the dojo, some of our fellow students wished us luck. I preferred to rely on my skills but welcomed their wish for one of life's lucky bounces to come our way.

Unlike the evening of the Run, this pretest had more the flavor of a traditional test—complete with no talking, bowing at all the right times, and plenty of "yes,

Sensei's." While the other guys made small talk before Joe and his black belts arrived, I tuned into my breathing pattern. This always helps me stay centered. Somehow, I always had this ability to retreat into an inner world, like when I conjured that mountain pool image during my first test with Joe—the one that got disturbed by that dead fly on my nose. It soothes me and allows me to keep a lid on the tension of the moment.

Soon we heard the dojo door close, and Joe told us to line up in the four corners of the center area. Joe gave us numbers (I was number 3, Dan was 1, Steven was 2, and Dave came last at 4) and said that he would not refer to us by name—only by our number.

As we expected, Joe started us with the various individual kata, which we did together. We stayed in formation fairly well throughout this part of the exercise. Joe emphasized the need for us to keep our stances low—harder to do when your quads start to fry—our movements crisp, and our kiais loud.

Then he lined us up again in our box pattern of four. Time for continuous kata. He told us we would have to do this for one hour. No breaks. Plus, if we started to slack off on the quality of our movements, he warned us that he would start asking us questions. This did not signify a break to stop and answer his inquiries. He meant we had to reply as we did the forms.

This greatly increases the difficulty of staying focused on doing your current form, because he asks you stuff about *other* kata. This reminded me of times during my eighth grade year when my drum instructor would purposely start a conversation with me as I played. To avoid having this dual task (speaking/singing and playing) screw up my playing, I spoke in time with the beat I had going. I never truly learned how to do it any other way.

Now, we could not get off so easily. We had to bury our katas so deeply into our muscle memory that we could continue doing it effectively while our minds went somewhere else. Naturally, the easier path entailed doing our forms so well to prevent Joe from even asking us any questions. But since Joe probably planned on doing it any way, the safest route involved getting your kata down so cold you could talk about other things.

Then came the twist. Before we started, Joe told each of us to start from different angles—not all facing straight ahead—which relieved us of the burden of keeping up with each other. But it meant we would do a repeat of our fool's fire drill we encountered the first time we practiced together. Good thing we experienced that kind of chaos before, or we would have constantly crashed into each other.

In prior tests, some of the black belts liked to stand in your way as you did your form. This placed you in a slight dilemma: are you supposed to work around that person, or do you smash your way through them like they didn't exist? One guy testing for an advanced belt rank unwittingly answered that question for us when he knocked over a black belt.

The reason why you need to work around each other during katas seems obvious now: in combat, your environment often changes, and you need to have a peripheral sense of such changes so you can adapt to them—but sometimes in a test, you panic. That guy panicked and made the wrong decision. Oh, it was so wrong!

Again, I felt pretty good about my forms that night, and I think Joe asked me one or two questions that didn't throw me off. My legs and feet burned by then end of the hour, but otherwise, I held up okay.

Next came an old kata called 10 Point—theoretically from the original system that predated the Shaolin monks. Other than the original sidestep into a training stance, your feet stay planted until you bow at the end. But it contains many blocks and strikes done in slow motion while you apply isometric tension (simultaneously making movements and resisting the very same moves).

This time, however, Joe had his black belts apply the tension. So if you can picture yourself standing in a deep stance with your feet apart, these black belts held and pushed against your arms as you executed all the techniques. That drill lasted an exhausting twenty minutes. My right shoulder felt like it had caught fire—I could feel the pain radiating down my right arm, but it somehow held up.

Joe had us line up again in our box pattern and await his next instruction. He asked us each to share our opinion about what we believed to be our best form. Then he went around the room again to see what we thought was our worst form. This question felt loaded, and the impulse struck me that maybe he wanted us to yell out, "I am prepared for this test, Sensei, and, therefore, I have no worst form!" But then he could pick apart that bravado in no time. You should be confident in his tests, but if you get cocky, Joe will expect you to back it up. By our rank, he wants you to interpret forms and techniques for yourself, but he demands that you're making sense from a martial perspective.

In the end, we all wisely chose to cite a best and worst form, and we each had to explain why we made these choices. I actually listed 10 Point, despite my shoulder's earlier protests, as my best kata, and something called 3 kata as my worst. In a sense, these reflected more of my personal preference than my disparate ability to do either form well. Bottom line, if my 3 kata sucked, I wouldn't have passed the brown belt test a few years earlier.

Finally, Joe gave us some general feedback about our katas and how he would watch our improvements in them over the weeks to follow. Then he bowed us out and dismissed us, just like that.

Overall, I not only felt good about my own performance that evening, I thought we worked well together as a group. As I drove home later, a brief wave of excitement rushed through me. For the first time since we started this trek back in April, I actually started to sense that I could make this climb to the summit. Bag Night, here we come!

Chapter 21

Bag Night

A couple of the other guys complained that their stomach, shoulder, and back muscles ached the next few days after Kata Night. But I felt surprisingly okay at that point—at least no worse than I felt after many other heavy training sessions—and I went into the next week's classes with a newfound enthusiasm.

Where Kata Night provided encouragement, however, I had my concerns about Bag Night. With only three weeks to go before that pretest, my big question centered around my shoulder, not so much my techniques or conditioning level.

Having had rotator cuff surgery on *both* of his shoulders, Dave had already arranged with Joe a modified version of Bag Night for him to undertake. The high numbers of punches we had to throw at pads and the heavy bag made this pretest especially risky for him. He didn't want to blow out a shoulder and have to drop out before Hell Week. And frankly, I had similar concerns.

Before the test, my shoulder only hurt a little if I moved it in certain directions. Already one cortisone injection and a round of physical therapy later, the ache grew worse and more consistent. With a fully torn cuff, this raised serious questions in my mind about my going the distance. After all, I still had the most potentially punishing part of the test to go.

One day, I spoke to Joe about this issue in his office. He understood and said that I could do the same thing he planned for Dave to do. "But," he said, "you may want to wait until we get closer to that night and see how your shoulder feels before you decide—because in a way, the stuff Dave's gonna do will be harder."

Sensing that Joe intended to send me a message, I kept my mind open to the idea of trusting my shoulder to get me through Bag Night. To stack the deck in my favor, I maintained a between-workout regimen of ice packs, anti-inflammatory pills, and physical therapy with Woody. Something about Woody's down-to-earth encouraging style helped calm my fears that I might inadvertently cause permanent damage to my right shoulder.

Back at the office, a new client, a figure skater, discussed his bafflement over getting stuck on a specific compulsory jump in his routine. He felt confused about how he could perform this jump previously and could still do more difficult maneuvers. But now, every time he tried to hit that specific move, he would bail out of it—either by resorting to a simpler jump or skipping it entirely.

In skating, the long road to a national title involves mastering a series of jumps of increasing difficulty. They call these jumps compulsory because skaters can't compete at the higher levels without successfully performing them in their routines. So my skater's problem had literally threatened to derail his plans to medal at the Olympics someday. To make matters worse, the harder he would push himself to get over it, the more anxious he would get even about the moves leading up to that specific jump.

I've seen this happen to skaters, gymnasts, and even myself in karate. It seems to occur because the move, once learned, must drop out of your conscious control and into your so-called muscle memory. This frees your mind to attend and react more efficiently to what's going on around you, instead of internally micromanaging your technique.

Depending on your confidence level—in yourself as an athlete but perhaps, more specifically, in your ability to perform a particular skill—you may have varying degrees of trust in letting your body do what it knows how to do. The lower your trust in things at least eventually turning out all right, the greater the chance that your conscious mind will want to rush in and take over.

Unfortunately, this mistrust leads to something known as overthinking or, more sarcastically, paralysis by analysis. At best, this causes a less fluid execution of the move, because you now must process both nonverbal and verbal information *simultaneously*.

In John Mahoney's book The Tao of the Jump Shot, he makes this point from a Zen perspective:

> The chief obstacle to perfection in the art and spiritual life is precisely the cognitive function of the mind . . . Whether one is wielding a sword, shooting an arrow, or shooting a basketball, the secret of perfection is to let events take their course without the thinker and thought intervening. (p. 13)

On the other hand, when you have a technique down cold, your analytical mind stops acting like an annoying back-seat driver. It essentially backs off, because it trusts that your body knows how to get it done. At its deepest, this higher self-trust allows for mistakes, especially during earlier stages of learning. I have noticed that confident athletes don't always expect positive results—only that with time they will eventually achieve them—and all will become right again with their universe.

So paradoxically, my skater needed to try *softer*, not harder. He had to find a way to mentally reduce the negativity associated with a botched jump. For him, blowing this move got equated with derailing his skating career. This prospect daunted him and caused his well-intended mind to try and intervene directly, instead of taking a more patient trusting approach. Ironically, *his own mindset* became a key obstacle to his goal attainment. I basically told him he needed to start treating himself better so he could start believing in himself again.

I've had to take a similar tack myself in sports. My ankle injury at nineteen led to a shattering of my confidence as a college hoop player. Confronted with my rapidly evaporating self-trust, I abandoned my own sense of myself and turned more to my coaches and teammates for validation. Predictably, this resulted in a downward performance spiral. I became nervous and insecure on and off the court, and my game never recovered the same sharpness.

Drawing from my experience, I know that doubting and punishing yourself over a lack of progress does not help rebuild your self-confidence. In fact, I am certain that it has the opposite effect. So now in karate, if I have trouble throwing a left hurricane kick because I'm not rotating around enough to pull the technique off, I deliberately avoid the temptation to get hypercritical or angry with myself.

Instead, I get curious. As my clients will tell you, I like to say—aloud if necessary—"Well, isn't that interesting!" Then I follow that with, "I wonder how that happened, and what I can learn from it." I know it sounds crazy, but my clients and I tend to find this a far more constructive way to handle setbacks—much better than hurling swears and insults at yourself—because it preserves your self-respect while you figure out how to get back on track.

Olympic speed-skating legend Bonnie Blair personifies this approach. In a recent interview, she confided that after a disappointing performance, she only focused on what went well that day. Instead of dwelling on her mistakes, as most athletes do following a loss, Blair preferred to keep her eye on her strengths. She said that this helped her maintain a high confidence level and that later on she would address her shortcomings in future training sessions.

Bonnie Blair credits her father's unswerving faith in her ability with helping her learn how to believe in *herself* even in the presence of adversity. She learned how to trust herself by *feeling* that trust from her father. Sadly, many people don't experience that kind of love and respect from the adults in their lives. This points to the critical role played by leaders in our society, such as coaches, teachers, and parents for developing the confidence of our youth.

In terms of leadership styles, the firm but fair leader easily outperforms the tyrant in the long run. And I think that the difference between tough love and tyranny boils down to their respect for your dignity and self-worth. Even if they do not think much of your performance, coaches and teachers must avoid insulting or humiliating you to drive their point home. Tactics like these should stay in the Middle Ages, where they belong; there's far too much research available pointing to the negative effects of such methods.

Phil Jackson, the famous NBA coach, seems to echo this idea in his autobiographical book, *Sacred Hoops: Spiritual Lessons of a Hardwood Warrior*. He says that he used to beat himself up after losing a game and that his mental approach had put him on "an emotional roller coaster" that tore him apart and hurt people around him. Eventually, he learned to steady his emotions by keeping the game of basketball in perspective; and that this ironically made him a better player, coach, and person.

The best coaches and teachers I ever had—and I count Joe among them—expected a lot from me and held me accountable for my mistakes. But they always stopped short of putting me down personally. And I think we should treat ourselves the same way. "Be your own best coach," I tell my clients. On that point, I'd like to think I lead by example.

As Bag Night approached, my shoulder felt no better or worse, so I told Joe I'd prefer to go through the standard pretest instead of Dave's modified protocol. Steven and I agreed to meet for an extra session over the weekend before the big event. Dan had an overnight patrol shift, so he planned to sleep the afternoon we met.

When I arrived at the dojo, Steven waved to me from the weight room area. He lifted very consistently and had bulked up a lot—his body looking quite different from the skinny kid we knew a couple years earlier. His daily stretching also gave him significant flexibility for a young man his size and height, which by then approached six feet two inches. Despite a genuinely pleasant demeanor, Steven carried an edge of intensity not far from the surface. This Harvard-bound kid had something to prove to the world, you could feel it.

Not surprisingly, Steven had also become a formidable sparring partner. That afternoon, I saw why. He had already designed a bag routine for us to practice. The heavy bag swayed slightly from the dojo ceiling, and the fire engine red air shield and focus mitts lay nearby on the carpeted floor. He said that he, Annette, and his father often came down to the dojo on weekends to do boxing drills—which explains why Rob nearly always peppered me with punches whenever I let him in too close when sparring.

Since I entered the martial arts via tae kwon do, which emphasizes kicks over punches, I never spent much time developing my hand strikes. Even today, I consider my long legs my weapons of choice when sparring. Steven and I simulated the drills that we imagined would make up our routine on Bag Night—alternating between the heavy bag, air shield, and focus mitts. Besides pushing my aerobic envelope, I got better with my hands that day because of Steven.

Thursday, June 22, 2000, Bag Night

After a grueling Thursday-night open class at Joe's, we all went downstairs to change out of our soaked gis. Joe told us we didn't need to wear our traditional gi tops for this pretest. In a sense, this made it feel more like the Run; plus, we could communicate with each other during the event. In fact, we had to coach and pump each other up during the various drills. Looking back, this had a remarkable effect on the focus and morale among the four of us that evening.

Dave got assigned a series of sparring techniques and forms to perform continuously throughout the entire night. While this meant he didn't have to summon the bursts of energy we needed during bag drills, we got rest periods between our sprints. Not Dave, he had to keep plugging away up and down the length of dojo floor all night. Every time we got a chance to catch our breath that evening, we glanced over at Dave and felt a combination of exhaustion and gratitude that we didn't have to do what he was doing.

Of course, this did not mean that Dan, Steven, and I got off much more easily either—just a different form of pain. Here's what we got to do that evening: first, Dave's absence left us with an uneven number of participants. This meant that we could not match up and rotate partners like we did on other pretests. Instead, Joe assigned us to one of three positions in the rotation: hitting the heavy bag, hitting the focus mitts or air shield, and holding the mitts or shield. Besides the brief breaks between rounds, the latter position would afford us an additional chance to recover aerobically throughout the night. But you couldn't just zone out while holding for your partner. Joe said the holder should also coach and push the other guys as they began fading in style or intensity.

We started off with me on the heavy bag, Steven hitting the focus mitts, and Dan holding for him. To protect our knuckles and wrists, we all wore light boxing gloves and wrist wraps. This came in especially handy when hitting the heavy bag, which weighs around one hundred pounds and doesn't move much when you punch it. Hit it hard at the wrong angle, and you can break your hand or wrist, even with gloves and wrist wraps.

For most of the night, all rounds lasted two minutes, which doesn't seem very long. But take my word for it, they add up when there's only a minute's rest between them. The first set of rounds focused on hand techniques, like jabs, reverse punches, hook punches, upper cuts, forearms, ridge hands, back fists, and spinning back fists. This part most concerned me, especially on the heavy bag, because I didn't want to blow out my right shoulder. I concentrated on good technique, and I initially held a little power back on my right.

Moving over to my next assignment, holding for Steven, required that I take off my gloves to put on the focus mitts. The holder got no extra time to do this or to put his gloves back on afterward so he had to move fast within the allotted minute break. I had a little trouble fitting my large hands inside the mitts, because the wrist wraps bulked up my paws to make for an even tighter fit. By the time I got finished switching gloves for mitts or vice versa, the break ended and I had to begin the next round. By the second circuit, the wraps started unraveling off my hands, rendering them more of a liability than an asset. With no time to fix them, I decided to yank them off completely in the third trip around—figuring I'd rather take my chances on a busted hand than not make it to the next station on time.

    The second set of rounds involved kicks—namely, front kicks, roundhouses, side and backkicks, and spinning kicks—followed by combinations of kicks and punches on the air shield and heavy bag. While this would reflect a part of the program for me to dazzle everyone with my kicking techniques, it takes more energy to lift your legs than your arms, and I started running out of gas. Nevertheless, Steven and Danny took turns goading me into making the pads pop with every foot strike. I reciprocated by cheering them on when they started sagging.

    Joe surprised me when he then announced that we had reached the last round. It constituted a three-minute final blast out on the heavy bag with whatever you had left in your body. Punches, kicks, head butts—any kind of strike you could think of, but you needed to throw a minimum number of leg techniques. This guarded against our conserving any energy by only using hand strikes. It may sound silly, but that stipulation makes a difference when your tank's empty, and you're functioning only on fumes.

    Sensing the end was near, we all screamed at each other to give it all up that round. I remember feeling the adrenaline rush and starting out hard. *Bam! Bam!* Dancing, switching my stance, then exploding with another combination, and feeding off Dan and Steven's hoarse voices. Then the reality of the toll taken on my body earlier on began to set in with about a minute left. Dragging through that last minute, I recall head butting the bag and hanging on to it so I wouldn't fall on my face. My legs and arms were complete Jell-O by the time Joe called, "Time!"

    Steven went last, and I saw the same urgent need in his face halfway through this final round for this all to end. When Joe stopped Steven, he also signaled Dave to cease his marathon demonstration of techniques and kata (which I'm sure he kept doing involuntarily in his head all night at home). We all dropped to the floor in a half circle around Joe and the other black belts and sucked down as much liquid as possible. Joe proceeded to congratulate us on our performance that evening, saying that we passed the "gut check" that it partly represented. Before he dismissed us, though, he had one more task for us.

    He told us we each had to complete a written essay over the next week. Everyone got a different question to answer, and we had to hand it in by that next Thursday's class. Dan's question had to do with the meaning of kata and its place in the study of the martial arts. Steven had to comment on the wisdom of having a strategy in terms of martial arts and life. Dave got a chance to write about the relative advantages and disadvantages associated with studying martial arts at different points in the age spectrum. And Joe asked me to explore the physical and mental qualities of a great martial artist.

Hmm, the qualities of a great martial artist, I thought to myself as I got into my car, *interesting*. On the drive home, I felt tired from Bag Night and relieved to have completed another pretest. But mostly, my mind locked onto the new challenge I sensed Joe had crafted specifically for me. He *knew* I could comment extensively on this subject, given my sport psychology background and penchant for philosophical discourse.

Chapter 22

Technique Night

Fueled by the high of Bag Night and by my intrigue with the essay question Joe assigned me, I dropped my gym bag in the kitchen and started scratching out the ideas that swirled around in my head all the way home. By 2:00 AM, my eyes got too blurry to read my own handwriting. I took a quick shower and crashed into my bed, completely spent. Pilar awoke and asked how I did. "I made it; we all did," I said groggily before slipping into a sweet coma.

Fortunately, I wised up about scheduling early appointments on days after pretest nights, so I let myself sleep in until nine the next morning. After eating a big breakfast and checking my voice mail, I fired up my PC to start writing. For some reason, I felt compelled to jump right back into the essay I began the night before.

Regretfully, I failed to show the same focus on writing the second edition of that sport psychology book chapter I had agreed to do with my original coauthor. I had initially cranked out my first draft only a little behind the deadline set by our editor. Now, I needed to do several revisions and simply had no time to fit the writing in between karate, my practice, and the health products business. My coauthor's patience had begun wear thin. Something had to go, and I knew it.

The decision to shut down my second business seemed obvious. I had not turned a profit in the nearly two years since I started the venture. The book chapter simply had to be done: it represented my credibility among my peers in sport psychology—which had taken many years to cultivate and would always remain a high priority in my professional life. But still, I balked at the idea of giving up on the second business.

As for family and friends, my enormous time crunch afforded me only precious few moments with Pilar and Evan—let alone my sister, brother, parents, or friends. And as patient as they had all been, I knew that I could not always put them last on my crazy agenda.

After exhausting all the options, I ended up just plain exhausted. My life floated along in an overstuffed basket tethered to a hot air balloon. With my weighty obligations crowded around me in that basket, all I could do was navigate the formidable currents of my world. And even though I pumped all my energy into that balloon to stay aloft, I felt myself descending slowly but steadily over the impending treetops just below.

Right next to me sat a heavy box loaded with nutritional supplements and other tools of my second business. Despite their financial value and all I had done to accumulate these items, I could no longer afford to carry the burden that that business had come to represent in my life. To avoid crashing, I had to heave that box overboard, enabling me to climb back to a safer altitude.

I notified my friend and colleague in the business of my decision to quit. Like having a weight lifted from my chest, the relief I felt came instantly. I had now reallocated my energies to focus more on the practice, my loved ones, the book chapter, and, of course, karate.

Monday, June 26, 2000

I awoke early that morning to put the finishing touches on my essay, which I planned to turn in to Joe that day. My schedule later that week looked hectic, so I saw no reason to wait until Thursday to hand it in. It ended up running nearly three pages, single-spaced, and I placed the document neatly on Joe's desk before heading into work.

I returned to the dojo later that day to attend class and bumped into Joe coming out of his office. He had already read my essay and said he really liked it. "It was so good, Rawb, that I could pass you to black right now," Joe gushed, way out of character for him during a test period—where he usually assumes this game-faced, stern persona. "But I won't!" he had to add quickly.

Then he just stood there grinning coyly for a few seconds, perhaps feeling satisfied that he had made his point without going overboard.

I scanned his face a moment before chuckling to myself, smiling back, and thinking, *There, now that's the Joe I know and love.* I knew Joe would never let me—or anyone—skip Hell Week. In fact, as much as I dreaded the pain of what lay ahead of me, I would have felt guilty and, strangely enough, disappointed.

For one thing, if Joe did pass me on the spot like that, most people would think he let me off the hook. I didn't want the question of favoritism floating around and particularly in the eyes of my comrades, who still had another month to go. That would definitely have confused them and dampened their morale. Besides, I couldn't envision any better ending to this test than to have us all cross the finish line *together*.

Yet Joe runs the show, and if he seriously thought anyone satisfied his requirements to pass his black belt test before its scheduled conclusion, he would do it with clarity and resolve. In my case, however, I wasn't there, and I knew it. But because of Joe's strongly held view of the black belt as a state of mind as well as an indication of superior physical skill, his praising my essay said to me that at least he believed I *thought* like a black belt.

He also added that after the test, I should seriously consider submitting my essay to *Black Belt Magazine*, one of the premier martial arts publications. Feeling very flattered, I had a great class that night—winning every point-sparring match; yep, I was on a roll.

As an aside, Joe's good-natured chiding that night did touch on a sensitive issue existing in the martial arts world—the seemingly inconsistent criteria for promoting people to black belt. Because certain systems pass students of lackluster ability to black, this hurts the credibility of all highly qualified martial artists bearing the same rank.

It boils down to the emotionally charged issue of what you can call an expert, since earning a black belt in any style usually presumes a high level of expertise. And because of the need for a largely arbitrary cut-off point in terms of skills attained, the line gets pretty blurry, depending on who you talk to. Unfortunately, when pressed to justify a given set of standards, the go-to response of the grand masters of various styles has often amounted to, "Because I said so." Not a constructive reply in any setting but especially underwhelming when you consider the titanic egos typical among the martial arts elite.

In Joe's case, this issue never comes up. His extraordinary reputation for high standards with his students, no matter who you are, eliminates any question about your karate competence within martial arts circles.

Thursday, July 13, 2000, Technique Night

I got to sleep the night before later than I preferred, because of a speaking engagement I had committed to do several months earlier. When I agreed to speak about sport psychology to the membership of an exclusive country club that prior February, July 12 seemed miles away. Back then, I hadn't even known about the black belt test. But because the club vigorously publicized my talk to its members and because marketing my services in front of many wealthy people made good business sense, the show had to go on.

The show went well, according to the club's program organizer, and I arrived home around midnight. The next morning, I recall hearing classical music in my dream and then awakening to the realization that the melody was actually coming from my radio alarm clock. As I grew more alert, I heard the music through a layer of static because the tuner hadn't quite zeroed in on 102.5, our local classical music station.

My stomach tightened as I remembered the challenge that lay ahead of me later that evening. I hadn't felt that anxious about a pretest since the Run. How simple that part of the test now seemed comparatively. The difference seemed like those times when you're an adult amused at something you took so seriously as a teenager. Perhaps someday, I'd look back at Technique Night and possibly the whole test itself with the same perspective that age brings. But it's hard to bear that in mind when it's actually happening to you.

Periodic waves of concerns about this pretest began to ripple across my consciousness that morning, competing for my attention. As I got my son ready for day care that morning, I had to suppress thoughts like, *What's Joe got planned for us? Can I make it through this one? Will the shoulder hold up?* And my favorite refrain, I would think, *This is the one that people most often flunk out of before Hell Week, most often flunk out, most often flunk.* I recall bursting the bubble of such worrisome thoughts by countering with something like, *Get a hold of yourself, Rob, you wouldn't be here right now if Joe didn't think you could do it.*

Pilar would pick Evan up that afternoon. This came as a relief because I wouldn't have to worry about him en route to the dojo. On other nights where I had classes, I had to arrange babysitting for Evan—or I'd hand him off to Pilar like a thirty-five-pound relay baton after she completed her workout at Esposito's. However slim the time margin this routine left for us, it generally worked okay during the test.

When I didn't have class, Evan watched me practicing kata or punch techniques in the living room while munching on dinner in his high chair. I can still picture his face covered with SpaghettiOs, giggling uncontrollably after I did a drill or delivered a kiai (subdued to avoid scaring him). One day, I shared this with Joe, and he said that he understood—because watching my techniques had the same effect on *him*. I walked straight into that one, and Joe probably couldn't resist.

After stowing Evan's backpack inside his cubby at day care, he planted a huge smooch on my cheek before joining his friends. Although completely oblivious to my preoccupations at that moment, Evan took the edge off my nerves with his hug and kiss. For him, that kiss had simply become part of his daily ritual—his way of saying good-bye and of easing his worry about spending the day away from his home. For me, on that day especially, it reminded me that regardless of what happened that evening, all would be right with the universe.

My day at the office sped by in a blur, and I got out a bit earlier than planned courtesy of my last client's late cancellation. Normally, that would tick me off, and I might charge that person for not leaving me enough time to offer the appointment hour to someone else. Not that day—the news actually came as a relief. So I rescheduled my client and left for Esposito's to go over my material with the guys before class.

We all seemed a little edgy that afternoon. Nobody knew what to expect. Leaving no stone unturned, we practiced all our techniques backward, forward, sideways (really—just in case we had to perform them from a sparring stance), and receiving left-hand attacks (as opposed to right-handed attacks, standard for our system). To avoid becoming another highway statistic, we wanted to stand ready for anything Joe could throw at us.

Thursday-night class went by quickly. That didn't stop me from feeling a strong sense of anticipation that entire hour. I struggled to constructively harness the energy that welled up through my gut. After class, the other students made small talk and joked with each other in the locker room. The four of us quietly changed our gis for the next round of entertainment. The others were done for the night. Our evening had only just begun.

Joe and his black belt assistants bowed us in and warmed us up again by having us do our basic hand and foot strikes at full speed. Afterward, he asked us to pull some mats into the center of the dojo. Joe paired us off and told us to stand in a box formation, facing our partners. Two of us stood on the mats, and the other pair would do their technique on the hard dojo floor.

The person standing on the mat about to do his punch technique would call it aloud before yelling, "Go." After everyone completed that one, the same guy would tell everyone to get up. We would then rotate our positions counterclockwise and reset for the next technique with a new partner. As soon as everyone settled into horse stances, the guy moving into the same spot on the mat as the first person who yelled, "Go," would call out the next technique. Naturally, Joe kept the pace crisp.

We went on until we exhausted our list of fifty punch techniques. This drill tested our concentration, because we learned many of these techniques in somewhat different orders. And since we could not repeat any techniques during that round, we had to think ahead before jumping into that yeoman's spot—or else you could easily freeze or call something off we already did, which might force us to start the entire drill over. With a long night ahead of us, botching instructions early on wouldn't bode well for our passing this pretest.

Another factor we needed to consider, however, involved Dave's and my shoulder situations. Joe told us we should call out the techniques that contained flips and hard falls when Dave or I could land on the mats. This, of course, required us to go beyond the simple recall of our orders: we had to quickly discern how the specific technique *ended* to make sure it didn't represent a potential problem for Dave or me.

It's not that Dave or I could *never* do any of these techniques on the hard floor. We did them in class fairly often, in fact. But because we had to go very hard and fast—and because we still had to stay healthy for another couple of weeks—Joe's instruction served as both a safety precaution and mental test (throughout his system, Joe has countless clever ways like this to simultaneously assess your physical and mental capacities).

In preparing for this night, the most common strategy we used involved writing all our techniques down on paper. This included every detail—from the opening footwork and block as the opponent strikes, to the final counterstrike, where we would yell our kiai. It seemed like the most logical approach to completely immerse ourselves in the myriad of techniques Joe expected us to know.

But writing it all out also forced us to get better at verbally describing what we do at any given point. And therein lay another major purpose for this entire test: not only to demonstrate our worthiness as students but to prepare us as teachers of the kenpo karate system.

As future spokespersons of the martial arts, we had to know how to articulate every aspect of what we teach in terms that students could understand. After all, knowing these special skills doesn't do you much good if you can't pass them on to the next generation of nascent practitioners.

My companions and I made it through the first set of drills but barely, it seemed. Joe gave us a ration of shit about not showing the level of intensity that he expected during a test. He dismissed us for a break to rehydrate and rethink our commitment to going our hardest—to hold nothing back.

We knew this meant Joe didn't like what he saw, and that that was, well, bad. Downstairs in the locker room, we guzzled liquids and blurted breathless encouragements to each other between swallows. Somewhere in the back of my head, I felt a strange sense of reassurance that our dismissal at that point didn't necessarily mean we were in immediate danger of flunking this pretest. So I tried to steer our thoughts to a few things we could do to improve our performance after Joe called us back in.

Nobody else seemed too frazzled or flustered either—so we seemed in good shape as a group when we got the cue from Steve's dad, Rob, to head back upstairs into the dojo. I do recall, however, a dull but detectable fear in my gut about how long this evening could last. A small cramp had developed in my right calf, and I didn't know if it would give me any serious trouble late in the game. I just hoped that I rehydrated enough during our break to keep that cramp at bay.

After bowing back in, Joe had us line up for a drill that we knew called monkey in the middle. This exercise involves having three people in a row, with the folks on either end facing each other, and the middle guy (the monkey) pointed one way with their back to the other person.

An exercise stolen from a schoolyard keep-away game, the monkey in the middle of this drill must move constantly back and forth to confront the guys on either end. The end guys serve as ukes and attack the monkey—who must then execute defensive and counterattack techniques. As soon as the monkey finishes off one attacker, he or she must pop back up on their feet and turn around for the next oncoming assault.

If that drill sounds exhausting, it is, particularly for the monkey. Not that the end guys can slack off—they must sustain the counterstrikes and slams to the ground and then jump right back up for their next turn while the other attack takes place. But the monkey bears the greatest mental strain, as they must block out their dizzying fatigue and stay focused on Joe's instructions to perform the right techniques. In contrast, the attackers can afford to go on autopilot and just crash and bash. Since we had a fourth guy, he had to perform his techniques against an imaginary opponent and then rotate into the drill on Joe's signal.

We did this and other similarly draining drills for what seemed like the next hour. During this time, Joe got to see how well we could execute our various techniques against punches, clubs, knives—you name it. He also saw how we handled changes in the directions and angles of attacks.

An unexpected dilemma that seemed to develop for us all had to do with how hard we were willing to hit each other. Joe quickly sensed our ambivalence, and he warned us several times that we needed to go all out. We all had apparently pulled our punches somewhat throughout the night.

Perhaps we feared that we might injure our comrades. Or that we might escalate our intensity too high and run out of gas. Either way, Joe would not accept less than 100 percent—he wanted to hear loud kiais and deep thuds sounding off our torsos when we got hit.

Joe assembled us for one last drill with the clear understanding that we had one last chance to go full blast. We could sense the night finally drawing to a close and that passing this pretest required us to hold nothing back. Dave came out swinging first, so intensely that it fired the rest of us up. His kiais sounded something like the rebel yell of a Confederate infantryman. He hit me so hard in the solar plexus area that I felt nauseous.

Luckily, I could still breathe. Still lying down, I recall smacking the floor hard with my fist—at that moment, I had to find a fast way to shift my attention away from the sick feeling in my gut. I needed to quickly channel my energy back into the drill. It worked, and I sprung up onto my feet ready for action, hardly missing a beat.

Despite the excited cheering from the black belts, we all started fading within minutes. Our legs wobbled, and our kiais and strikes began to lose their intensity. My leg cramp returned, but my overall bodily fatigue allowed me to ignore the pain. It had been a long night. Joe mercifully stopped the drill and told us to line up in our original box pattern. *We made it*, I thought to myself as I hobbled into position and stood at attention. I could feel my heart decelerating slowly with every breath. My body heat radiated through my sweat-soaked gi.

Before bowing us out for the night, Joe told us that we needed to design a form of our own that we would refine over the last few weeks of the test. The kata should take between one to two minutes to complete—no more, no less. He said we should get creative in developing this form and that it should showcase some of our strongest moves. Finally, we would also need to give a name to our new form.

We bowed, dropped to our knees to meditate for a moment, rose up to bow again, and then Joe dismissed us. The four of us stumbled downstairs again to the locker room for a quick rinse and headed back to our homes. It was 12:15 AM—we had been at it that night for four hours.

Hell Week and its inferno now beckoned us. Now, no matter what happened, this test of skill and spirit would conclude in just fifteen days. As football coaching great Lou Holtz once lamented, "It's not the end of the world, but I can see it from here."

Chapter 23

Eddie Died Last Night

Up until Technique Night, events in my life in and out of the dojo had gone roughly according to plan. But there are some things in life you just can't anticipate—some things that blindside you and knock you for a loop. That's what happened on Wednesday morning, July, 19, 2000, the week between Technique Night and Hell Week.

The phone rang in my office around 9:15 AM. Ordinarily, I would have already clicked off the ringer function on my phone to avoid interruptions during my meetings with clients. Ordinarily, that call would have sadly and quietly been routed into my voice mail. As I was about to discover, however, this was not going to be an ordinary day.

My 9:00 AM client had called apologetically at 9:10 AM to cancel her appointment that day. After rescheduling her session, I had just hung up the phone when Pilar's call came through. I picked up the receiver.

For years, my long work hours have meant that I haven't provided my wife the kind of support I perhaps had implicitly promised on our wedding day. All the same, on that day, I managed to be in the right place at the right time—eerily similar to the time when I walked into her apartment just after she had received the news by phone of her sister's unexpected death in 1990.

"Rob, are you in a meeting?" Pilar asked through a strained voice that instinctively told me to brace myself for some really bad news. "No, what's wrong?" I replied while my mind quickly groped at possibilities for who might've died. Pilar interrupted my silent guessing game with the words, "Eddie died last night." That was it; then she waited for my reaction.

In true oafish form, I blurted out, "Eddie who?" Of course, as soon as I asked that question, I knew she meant Eddie Diaz, one of her closest friends from college. But the news so stunned me that it took a moment to register that she was talking about *our* Eddie—the vibrant, warm, outrageously funny forty-one-year-old Eddie.

Nope. Eddie was nowhere on that possibilities list I'd hurriedly assembled in my mind just moments earlier. Before it all sank in, my subconscious made one more attempt to pretend that this tragedy did not really happen. "Eddie f—ing Diaz?" I asked as if to say, "Come on, Eddie's too young; you sure we're talking about the same guy?"

After finally regaining my emotional footing, I managed to ask how he died. "He had a heart attack while away on business; his body's still in Scotland. They're having some trouble getting the paperwork through to have him sent back home." My disbelief gave way to sadness. After consoling each other and reviewing some of the scant details Pilar had, we agreed to talk again later when we returned home from our offices.

But how do you go back to work when you just hear that you're never going to see your close friend again? I sat leaning with both elbows on my desk—my face sunken into my hands, momentarily oblivious to all else.

Memories of the last time I saw him flashed through my mind. He told me he loved me—no accompanying punches in the arm, no head noogies, just how he felt about me. Guys just don't volunteer this kind of stuff. But that was Eddie.

Besides his affectionate warmth, he was also sharp-witted. During a train ride from Venice to Paris in the fall of 1996, someone in our crew wondered aloud how to say "something stinks" in French. Eddie didn't hesitate a second before responding in a terrible French accent, "Why, Pepe LePew, of course." Vintage Eddie.

As the fog began to lift, I thought selfishly of Eddie's young age and how closely this signified my *own* fragile mortality. And more urgently, I wrestled with how Eddie's death and impending funeral could very well have meant my missing the final week of my karate test.

Yuck, it's all about your goals and needs, now isn't it Rob? I thought with a visceral wave of guilt. After all, this could nullify all my sacrifices to get this far into the test—one more week to go, and now the unthinkable happened. Go figure: I would have guessed my not succeeding would've been caused by an injury (as when I had to drop out of an earlier brown belt test) or crashing and burning during one of Joe's brutal pretests. But these self-absorbed thoughts quickly yielded to the acceptance that I couldn't miss Eddie's funeral. I left a message for Joe to call me.

Glancing quickly at the clock, I noticed that I had ten minutes to make the gargantuan leap required to focus now on helping others deal with *their* problems. Before doing so, I ached once again for Eddie, his one-year-old daughter—who would never know her sweet father—and his wife, Rosie, who I imagined would at that point be an utter basket case (in her place, I know I'd be one).

Startled by the phone, I quickly grabbed the receiver. Joe had returned my call. Unsure of what he would say, I somewhat sheepishly filled him in on my situation. I half expected him to share his condolences for my friend and for my having to bow out of the test at such a late stage.

To my surprise, Joe raised the possibility of rescheduling Hell Week. In fairness to the other examinees who may have had conflicts with pushing Hell Week back, however, Joe said I first needed to check with them before he would authorize the schedule change. Since nobody knew when Eddie's body would be sent stateside, we didn't know when the funeral would take place. In fact, at that time, we were told it might be weeks before he could be laid to rest.

After a quick trip to DC to check in on Eddie's family and with no further word on his solemn flight home, Pilar and I decided that I would enter Hell Week as scheduled. Nonetheless, I greatly appreciated Joe's compassionate gesture to accommodate my personal situation—despite his well-established reputation for rigidity when it comes to how he runs his tests.

Counting my tenth wedding anniversary, this was the second time he surprised me with his willingness to reasonably accommodate my personal circumstances. I should have begun to recognize by then that he actually *wanted* to see me pass this damn thing.

So I marched on solemnly but with determination into Hell Week.

Chapter 24

Hell's Door

Sunday, July 23, 2000

Flying to DC to comfort Eddie's stunned wife and extended family—who had flown in from Puerto Rico and Texas—took an understandable toll on us all emotionally. His lovely Alexandria brick home looked just the same way I remembered it from a visit just the prior February. Except now I had entered into some surreal parallel universe—a world where Eddie no longer existed. This was his place, but it wasn't his anymore. A very weird, sad feeling enveloped me the whole weekend we spent there.

Something else I could feel on the flight home was my shoulder and a nagging cough that had worsened over the weekend. Dr. Ross had given me another cortisone shot the day before I left for DC, but it didn't relieve the soreness I experienced since getting thrown around the dojo on Technique Night. *It's going to be a long week,* I thought to myself as I tried to fall asleep late Sunday night.

Monday, July 24, 2000

Light day at the office. I had some time between appointments to check in with my primary care doctor about that cough. Something told me I might need my bodily functions—especially my lungs—to run at full capacity. She said it wasn't strep throat, and I didn't appear to have pneumonia, but she sent me for a chest X-ray anyway.

The pictures came back clear, so my doc guessed at the diagnosis of a budding cold and sent me home. Only partially relieved, I left her office hoping things would clear up soon—real soon.

Earlier in this story, I mentioned the importance that dumb luck sometimes plays in determining the direction your life takes. This emerging cold started looking like one of those bad turns of fortune that could hurt me down the stretch.

I had my monthly meeting with Father John Ulrich at St. Anthony's Shrine in downtown Boston on that same Monday. As a Franciscan priest, Father John belongs to the far left wing of the Catholic Church. Inspired by their free-spirited patron, St. Francis of Assisi (a medieval city located in the Umbrian region of Italy), this order seems to sneak their message of acceptance and forgiveness under the Vatican's rigidly maintained radar field.

And John embodies this humble order. His laid-back, warm style immediately puts you at ease. He makes you feel like you could talk about anything and not get condemned to hell—not that I believe in the concept of hell as some fiery depository for "n'er do wells." In fact, I believe we created a hell partly to keep the ignorant masses in line and perhaps also to reflect the suffering we endure right here on earth. To me, at least, the very notion of the eternal superpowers God and Satan ruling over their respective kingdoms hardly seems much different from Greek and Roman mythology. It smacks of the monarchical black-white thinking so prominent in the years from which they first emerged.

In any case, I sought John's counsel with the hope that he wouldn't *tell* me how to think. Instead, I needed him to shepherd my own thought process as I struggled to grasp some deep spiritual questions that have resided in me my entire adult life.

Despite my sizing him up as trustworthy, I tested him in the opening moments of our first session. I shared with him my contempt for "godspeak," my label for when people lace their language with religious terms. It also covers when folks imply that God plays with us like puppets and back their viewpoints with blatantly flawed reasoning to explain life's tides of fortune.

A woman I had just overheard in St. Anthony's lobby provoked my tirade in John's office that first day. She had announced to the sleepy desk attendant that God was with her that morning. Then she went on to explain that she had slipped down her front steps but had somehow escaped unharmed. This astounded me—of all the plausible explanations for her not getting hurt during her fall, she zeroed in on the idea that *God* had spared her from injury.

To arrive at this conclusion, she needed to presume that God would actually take time out of His busy day—the same day in which thousands of helpless children around the world would die of starvation and disease, no less—to buffer her fall. She also had to completely ignore the fact that God surely could have prevented the whole damn incident altogether. Evidently, that never entered into her equation after taking her spill that morning.

"It just pisses me off," I added in a huff—half expecting John to lecture me on concepts such as tolerance and faith. But he just smiled and said matter-of-factly, "Yeah, that pisses me off too."

Thus began a warm relationship with a man whom I knew I could trust with my questions. Ironically, that woman and her screwball story became a conduit to my developing a strong personal connection with a man of God. And maybe through such deep, meaningful connections with others, we get the closest tangible glimpses of—dare I say—God's existence.

Looking back, I can see how my paths of spiritual, professional, and martial arts development had all intersected in a big way during that time in my life. Driving back from John's office, I felt a sense of trust and purpose about the direction of my life, including our test scheduled to take place in just a few hours.

7:15 PM—only forty-five minutes left before game time. Dan, Dave, Steven, and I nervously paced around downstairs waiting for the 7:00 PM class to end. This week, we would not have to attend classes before going under Joe's microscope.

We reviewed all our material but paid special attention to the large variations of basic hand and foot strikes in our repertoire. The numbers of strikes we know only become limited by the many-faceted surfaces of our hands, feet, knees, elbows, forearms, and forehead (yes, the thicker-boned area of the skull makes the forehead a bona fide weapon).

Joe said that our evening will begin with our running a pseudoclass, where we would take our classmates through all these types of strikes: starting with hands and arms first and then followed by leg and foot strikes. Again, we could not freeze and say nothing when called upon. Nor could we repeat the same strike called off earlier. This meant that while doing the strike called off before, you had to process your next choice, including a back-up strike to avoid duplicating an earlier call.

Worrying so much about missing any hand or arm strikes, we spent probably the first forty-five minutes calling off a ridiculous variety before Joe yelled at us. He seemed annoyed that we had not moved on to kicks. "Is this a system without kicks?" he asked, and we breathlessly barked back, "No, Sensei!"

Dave later told me that he felt discouraged at that point. He feared that if we went a shorter while before switching over to kick strikes, Joe would have confronted us about missing certain hand techniques. In other words, he worried that Joe had placed us in a no-win situation. My concern had to do with our going so hard on punches that we would have little energy left for our kicks. And as I mentioned, kicks were my specialty, so I wanted to show my best stuff.

Fortunately, in the end, neither of these fears came true—we had what it took to get through the night. We finished the evening by demonstrating our new kata, one by one in front of Joe and the other black belts. Joe had his stopwatch out to see if our katas conformed to his instruction for them to take between one to two minutes to complete.

Steven, probably the best overall athlete among us, designed a form that had several flying kicks, one or two tumbles, and lots of angular attacks. To the novice student, he would have looked like he got into a brawl on a Jackie Chan movie set.

Then Joe asked Steve what he had named his kata. *Named his kata?* I thought to myself, *shit, what am I going to name mine? All that preparation, and I never even thought of a name for it!* Steve, of course, had a name ready.

Dan's clear strength has always been his powerful hand strikes—you just hated having to take his punches to the gut. His form, therefore, had a lot of straight-ahead punches and kicks, and to me it resembled Sherman's March through Atlanta. Like me, Dan had not thought of a name for his kata (Sherman's March might have worked), so Joe said he'd give him a little time to think of one.

My form of course had lots of kicks—thirteen different types in total—and some unique hand strikes and meditative breaths inserted for good measure. The whole thing took about a minute and a half to do and followed a basic capitol I pattern on the floor. When I finished, Joe inquired about my kata's name, and (since I had more time than Dan to think of one) I proudly called it I Ching, named after the famous Chinese philosophical treatise. This conveniently fit both the spiritual symbolism I hoped to convey, along with its I pattern. I stood at attention somewhat pleased with myself for digging that title out of my ass under pressure. Yep, very clever title.

Except then Joe asked if I heard him specifically say on Technique Night that we shouldn't use an I pattern when constructing our katas—because he was looking for greater complexity in our forms. *Oh, man,* I thought to myself, truly surprised by his question. Maybe I spaced out at the end of Technique Night, but I totally missed that instruction—along with forgetting the part about naming your kata. In any case, I had no other choice but to tell Joe that I had not heard him say that. He sat there silently for a good while before dismissing me and calling on Dave.

Dave showed a conservative but well-rounded kata, containing a solid repertoire of his foot and hand techniques—yet allowing for his preference for the latter and accommodating his more limited range of leg flexibility. Dave walked away with the award for most creative kata name: Fifty-year Headache. This title captured both his age at the time, and it played on the name of one of our punch techniques called Ten-year Headache because it contains three substantial blows to the head.

Joe told us that we would be expected to fine-tune our katas all week, and he gave us each some suggested improvements before dismissing us for the night.

One night down and four more to go. We had just successfully passed through hell's door.

Chapter 25

Styx and Stones

Tuesday, July 25, 2000

The next day came too soon. I felt like I just drifted off to sleep when my alarm went off, and that damn classical radio station drop-kicked me into Tuesday. Despite the cooler forecast this week, Pilar had the AC on, and its hypnotic drone sounded like chants drifting from a distant Buddhist temple. That steady hum leveled out all other sounds, providing a protective auditory cocoon around us while we slept. That morning, 102.5's program manager had a sense of humor in choosing something perky by Tchaikovsky to pierce my consciousness.

As I stepped into the shower, my mind shifted to the events of the night before. Dave, Dan, Steven, and I had just crossed the River Styx. Forever emotionless, that boatman had already pulled away from shore. *No turning back now*, I thought as I toweled off and inspected my naked body in the mirror for scratches or bruises. Nothing serious on the surface, at least, but I rolled my sore shoulder around to gauge its stiffness.

I recall how wiry thin I looked by that time in the test. The past fifteen weeks had shaved my body-fat count down now probably to single digits. The subtler lines of my muscles and arteries had risen to the surface of my skin, and you could count my ribs from across the room. Ironically, I could afford to eat anything I wanted—say, two fatty steaks, a side of fettucine alfredo, and a Ben & Jerry's chaser—but I didn't really crave any of that stuff. My appetite had taken a backseat to my training, and I ate and drank mainly to refuel my taut frame. But I never doubted that my taste buds would return, and I made a promise to treat myself when this was all over.

Glancing through my Palm Pilot, I noticed that my schedule at the office seemed reasonably busy. A world-champion athlete made an appointment with me to discuss some personal issues. He suffered in the self-doubt department but had previously managed to keep his composure during competitions. His challenge surfaced primarily within his family and romantic life, but now it started affecting his sport performance.

We met in the early afternoon, and I liked that guy from the moment I met him. Aside from my respect for what he had accomplished athletically, he had a kind disposition, and you could tell he cared about people. And he *really* cared about his girlfriend—a sexual-abuse survivor who unfortunately had a nasty side that came out when she drank.

Having had a father who abused alcohol, my client never drank much himself. Perhaps because of his father, he learned how to function around damaged people. Always seeking to keep the peace, even as a kid, this guy would find himself taking verbal abuse from his father. And now he took it from his girlfriend. Despite her frequent apologies and promises of reform, her ongoing insults and confrontations—many times in public—had taken their toll on my client's self-esteem.

Whoever made up that sticks-and-stones saying really got it wrong when they proclaimed that words never hurt you. I see it all the time in my practice. Like a cancerous tumor, a loved one's malignant words can devour an otherwise healthy person from the inside out. I find it particularly hard to see this happening to kids.

Fortunately for my client, he made it through his own childhood fairly intact. Along the way, he had developed a solid support network and the personal resolve necessary to eventually bail out of that toxic relationship. Having subsequently found a healthier love interest, he came to me now for my perspective on how to regain trust in his own judgment—at least when it comes to matters of the heart.

I reassured him that his self-trust would heal on its own within the safe confines of a more loving, respectful relationship. Part of that healing, of course, would involve grieving the loss of his troubled ex-girlfriend. He needed to accept that while the relationship had failed, he could have done little to stop its destruction.

Over time, my client came to see his prior relationship as a melodramatic replay of his father's disapproval. No matter what he did in either relationship, he could never ensure his feeling loved and accepted. In our meetings, my client worked on developing more effective ways to prevent anyone, under any circumstances, from treating him with such disrespect.

In a strange way, my work with that young man smacked of the classic story of someone losing their honor and coming to a sensei to learn the martial way. Because of its widespread appeal, we see this theme resurface in many books and movies. In my practice, I often see the parallels between physical and verbal conflicts: you need to assess your adversary, decide to engage or withdraw, and select the best response depending on the circumstances. And perhaps most importantly, you must keep your composure. So my sessions with certain clients sometimes resemble lessons in "verbal martial arts."

I left the office around 5:30 PM. This gave me plenty of time to review my techniques and warm up before things heated up with Joe at 7:00 PM. Unfortunately, I spaced out and took the Mass Pike to the dojo, and traffic moved slowly. Boston earns its notorious reputation for traffic because of its geography and the inevitable laws of physics. Wedged against the Atlantic coast, there's no room for Beantown to expand. And like it or not, you just can't fit a million cars on a highway system designed to accommodate half that amount.

Then there are the "solar delays" you hear about in local traffic reports. On clear days, commuters face the bright glare of the morning sun on their eastward journey into Boston. On the way home, they must deal with solar blindness while heading west. That was my situation: setting sun causing lots of impatient drivers to choke the roadways and making me sweat the ride in to the dojo that evening. "Should have never taken the Pike," I cursed to myself while gripping my steering wheel.

Nevertheless, I made it there by 6:30 PM, somewhat ruffled, but ready to get down to business. I joined my comrades in the lower dojo, where they had already begun stretching. Unlike the first night of Hell Week, the mood in the room felt less grim. We even joked around a little before the show would begin in just a few minutes. Despite the nerves you feel before any important athletic event, I felt relatively loose, energized, and confident.

Dave had some lined notebook sheets spread out around him. He kept copious notes on every punch and weapon technique and every kata he had ever learned. The detail with which he described our system amazed me. He not only had the steps broken down into individual parts, he wrote reminders about the subtle nuances contained in each of those parts—details like, "Snap your head, and look before you turn to block your opponent's strike." Every move had to have clean, crisp lines and a clear purpose.

I recalled first seeing these cheat sheets back around Kata Night. We all appreciated having such a precise blueprint to cross-check how well we each grasped these subtleties. At the black belt level, we knew Joe would not accept a muddled understanding of the kenpo system—especially at the micro level.

We got the nod from one of the black belts that we needed to head up to the main dojo. Dave scooped up his notes, and we all grabbed our gear and hopped upstairs in our fresh gis and bare feet.

As if clairvoyant, Dave's sharing his notes on kata could not have been more dead on for what we needed to start off night two of Hell Week. After bowing us in and having us meditate briefly, Joe kicked off the night by running us through all of our kata. At an individual level, he looked for precise stances, crisp strikes and blocks, and red-hot intensity. As a group, he wanted us to hit all those moves and kiais together in unison—like we were one body, one voice.

He then called us out individually and picked specific forms for us to do. Following this, Joe had us show our own forms, which we unveiled for him the previous night. He wanted to see our consistency from the prior showing and also any improvements we made in our kata. Before it was my turn, Joe asked me if I chose to keep the parts in my kata at the beginning and end where I took three long breaths and what they meant.

"Yes, Sensei," I shouted, "each breath represents the different perspective you can have in a fight: yours, the opponent's, and the observer's, Sensei." I was careful not to look him in the eye, observing the Asian belief that doing so with a superior was disrespectful, which Joe would not tolerate. In prior tests, Joe would occasionally try to catch my eye with his movements, testing my concentration, but I always stayed focused on a point beyond him. Tonight was no different.

Joe also asked me if I kept the same title for my kata, and I told him that I modified it from simply "I Ching" to "I Ching Kick-line Kata." When he asked me about this change, I replied that this reflected the fact that my kata showcased the power of most of the kicks used within our system.

"How many different types of kicks are in your form?" Joe probed.

"Thirteen, Sensei," I responded.

"Name them," he shot back, challenging my resolve.

Running through my form in my head, I called each kick off sequentially as I visualized it. A nagging worry that I had somehow not counted the total number correctly competed for my attention as I responded carefully, "Front ball, spinning reverse crescent, crossover side blade, thrust, back, instep, side blade, hook, roundhouse, spinning back, wheel, axe, and stomp kick, Sensei!" I probably sounded sure, but inside I still wondered if I named them all.

After a pause, Joe seemed satisfied with my response and told me to do the form at his signal. I stood at attention, feet together, my flattened left hand resting on top of my right fist. My arms bent so my elbows bowed outward, with my hands nearly touching my solar plexus area.

Nodding slightly, Joe said, "Begin."

I bowed deliberately, and at the same time I pushed my fists away from my chest and expelled air through pursed lips, and then I returned to my upright stance at attention. A moment later, my right foot slid out about three feet while my hands dropped below my waist, opened, separated, and circled upward. They met—palms facing up, thumbs inward, and fingers together—at the same time my right foot stopped. Only the tips of my thumbs and first two fingers of each hand touched, creating a triangular window for me to peer through.

Next, I took in three deep, centered breaths. This matched the number of corners contained in my symbolic portal and, as mentioned earlier, the different perspectives you can have in a fight. With each breath, I directed my focus inward and felt my knees flex deeper, causing my body weight to drop lower in my stance. At the end of the third breath, I lowered my gaze and turned my attention outward to the battle about to ensue.

I readied myself by dropping my elbows down and shooting them out simultaneously behind me and then quickly crossing my wrists (left over right) as they rose up into a cross block (as if to stop a downward strike about to clobber my head). As my elbows returned hard and sharp to point back behind me, I yelled out a loud "kiai," and then I paused a moment before going on the offensive.

The following description illustrates the detailed sequence of events contained within my kata's story:

My imaginary opponent stands before me. He sends out a low punch to my groin, and I respond by stepping forward with my right foot and using a right downward pressing palm block. This causes him to lean slightly forward, and my blocking hand then shoots upward into a chicken-wrist strike (which uses the top of my wrist as the striking surface) to his chin. As he backs up, he sends out a weak rising kick, which I handle by stepping forward with my left foot and doing the same block-strike combination with my left hand.

Stunned, my opponent straightens up, and I pop him quickly in the solar plexus with a right-front ball kick. As he teeters forward again, I plant the ball of my right foot down in the center of his stance and spin 360 degrees around while I knock him out cold with a left spinning-reverse crescent kick that lands where his jaw meets his ear. My kiai accentuates the power of that kick to his head, and I end up in a fighting stance (clenched fists on guard) with my right foot closer to my fallen opponent.

Sensing further danger, I snap my head left and change my guard to face a new opponent attacking from the opposite direction. Others also approach, but I step in quickly with a left crossover side-blade kick into his solar plexus and a simultaneous left back fist strike to his left temple. As my left foot recoils and steps to his right, my left hand opens up and loops from the attacker's left temple over his head. Cupping the back of his head, I pull it toward me and let out a "kiai" as I drive his nose into his skull by smashing my right elbow into his face. He's done, but other attackers begin to close in on me.

After retracting my forearm and dropping the other guy to the ground, I sense the closest attacker 135 degrees to my right. Turning quickly, I see him coming at me and, I notice his right hip twitch toward me. Anticipating a right-footed kick, I step back with my right foot and draw both arms up—crossing my wrists (left over right) to make a downward cross block. I need to make it strong enough to deflect his powerful kick safely toward the ground between my feet.

The momentum of this guy's kick and my block forces his upper body to lunge toward mine. To stop him cold, I fire my hands upward—wrists still crossed—straight into his throat while stepping toward him with my right foot. The blow cracks his windpipe and stands him up straight. Keeping my wrists crossed, I raise my hands above his nose and open them into a rakelike shape. As I uncross my wrists, I slash my fingernails across his eye area, blurring his vision momentarily. I then draw my elbows back and disable him permanently by shooting a double-thumb strike, knuckle deep, straight into his eyes.

With no time to waste, I retract my elbows and turn ninety degrees right to find another attacker about to crush me with a front kick. By reflex, I quickly step back again with my right foot to give myself room to block his strike. I deliver the same cross-block-strike-rake combination, but I don't finish him off with thumbs to the eyes. Instead, after I uncross my wrists and rake his eyes, I cup both hands and slam them together on his ears—rupturing the drums. Stunned by the pain of my counterattack, the guy offers little resistance when I grab the hair behind his ears and yank his head toward me. My forehead smashes his nose in, and he collapses.

Two more down, three left—for now, at least. I turn another ninety degrees right; and that puts one guy directly in front of me, one behind, and the last guy to my direct right. This time, I can't finish one guy without getting hit hard by at least one other attacker. The key is to time my defensive moves for those closest to me at a particular moment.

In this case, the guy on my right was still a few steps away. I stop the advance of the one in front of me with a right thrust kick to his gut, and—keeping my weight on my left foot, I fire a backkick straight into the groin of the guy behind me.

Both guys double over from my first strikes. But they're still a danger to me, so I quickly follow up with two more kicks. I send a right instep kick upward into the jaw of the guy in front of me, snapping his head back and knocking him out on impact. My foot retracts, and I turn and deliver the same knockout blow with a right backkick to the second guy's head.

With no time to waste, I recoil my leg and shoot out a side-blade kick that luckily slips over the guard of the man on my right as he charges in. The momentum of his charge adds more power to my kick, enabling the edge of my foot to smash in his front teeth. I yell out a "kiai" on impact, and he topples over, moaning and semiconscious.

Because all five of these kicks must occur so quickly, my right foot never touches ground. This requires a firm balance on my left foot during the entire sequence. My right foot finally touches ground when I place it down in the direction of my last attacker. This also happens to complete my clockwise circle of defense against the last six guys—the first one being the opponent I dropped with my right elbow to his nose.

Hearing another attacker coming from my left, I change my guard and shuffle back to give myself some room to defend myself. At the same time, I redirect his oncoming right-side blade kick with a left downward pressing palm block. Rearing back on to my right foot, I clock him in the head with a lead-leg, left-hook kick to his left temple—his head snaps left, and the momentum of my kick carries my foot over it to the other side. Keeping my left leg up, I follow the hook with a roundhouse kick to his right temple.

These shots to his head daze him and cause him to open his stance and wobble. I quickly lower my left foot to the ground and step in with my right foot—sliding it around his right foot in a crescent-shaped path. At the same time I move in, I use a left palm block to avoid a defensive strike. My palm nudges his right fist away and opens him up for my next strike—a right back fist that starts below the waist and circles up and around—which hits his right temple just as my right foot comes to a stop behind his. He stiffens up, and for a split second, I stand parallel to but just in front and to the right of his shoulders.

Seamlessly, I slide my left foot behind my right into a stance perpendicular to his. At the same time, I draw my hands, fingers pointing toward each other, over his head and circle them abruptly around toward his chest and back. As my left foot comes to a stop, the heels of my palms slam simultaneously into his solar plexus and spine. The impact of this strike knocks the wind out of him, and he starts to bend forward. My left hand reaches up and pushes the back of his head downward while I open my right thumb and jam a right tiger's mouth strike (the striking surface occurs between the thumb and forefinger) up into his windpipe. This stops his forward momentum, and I finish him off with a neck break.

To do this, my left hand keeps holding onto the back of his head, and I slide my right hand from his throat to his chin. Then, I push his chin away sharply with my right hand while pulling the back of his head toward me with my left. This twists his cervical vertebrae, causing it to crack and sever his spinal cord—and, in all likelihood, killing him instantly. My kiai drowns out the popping sound, but I can feel the vibration of the bones breaking in my hands. He flops to the ground, and I see another attacker coming at me from my left.

My right hand, still extending out from my last strike, closes into a fist. I drop my stance a bit and twist right 180 degrees, avoiding his kick to my head, and I surprise him with a right spinning back fist that crashes into his right temple as my right foot stops near his. He stumbles over to his left, but another attacker closes in behind him. I push him away with a left thrust kick. As he advances, I step down with my left foot and deliver a right spinning backkick to his solar plexus and continue my rotation for a full 360 degrees. Stopped dead in his tracks, he bends over from the powerful blow to his stomach. This leaves his head open for the finishing blow—a 360-degree right spinning wheel kick delivered with a kiai—which fractures his skull and sends him rolling sideways to my right.

Directly in front and behind me approach two final attackers. The closer of them is in front, and he comes at me first, so I pop a quick right instep kick that tracks up the inside of his lead leg and into his groin; he grimaces and lurches forward. I quickly retract my foot and raise it over his right shoulder. At the moment, my right knee locks straight, my foot hangs two feet over the back of his head. Using my hamstring muscle, I drive the back of my right heel onto his skull like a hatchet into a wood block. The blow knocks him face down, and my right foot steps down near his right shoulder and arm.

I raise my left knee to step over the body of the first guy so I can turn to face my other attacker. On the way across, I quickly kiai as I stomp on the guy's spine with my left foot before touching ground by his opposite hip. The impact cracks his lumbar vertebrae and ensures that he will not rise up behind me as I defend myself against the other oncoming attacker.

From my right foot forward stance, I turn my attention to the other guy and notice an opening to his groin area. I fire the same sequence of instep-axe-stomp kicks but this time starting with my left foot and finishing with my right foot touching ground near his right hip.

I scan the area, pull my right foot back over the last attacker, turn left, and pivot back into a training stance facing in the direction where I had originally begun the entire kata. I conclude the form with a symbolic upward cross-block into a double elbows backward strike while screaming my final cathartic kiai. From that position, I raise my arms back up in circle them toward each other above my head—once again, forming the *I Ching* triangular portal with my thumbs and fingers.

Drawing three slow breaths, in through the nose, out through the mouth, I center myself and focus on slowing down my racing heart. After the last breath, I draw my feet together and circle my hands back around to the left-palm-over-right-fist position. My hands and feet meet simultaneously. From my upright stance, I bow and breathe outward while pushing my hands forward. The kata ends.

Returning to the upright stance, I stared straight ahead and wait at attention for my next instructions from Joe. "Number 3, back to the wall," he said after a moment's contemplation, "number 4 (Joe's reference to Dave), come on out."

The remainder of the night involved various tests of our material in other areas. Pretty straight-ahead stuff, and we were all on. By night's end, we felt like we all actually might pull this thing off. I drove home with a level of reassurance I had not yet enjoyed after stumbling out of any of Joe's tests—maybe because the end felt so close, or perhaps because I was deluding myself. Either way, two days down, three more to go.

Chapter 26

Living in the Fringe

Wednesday, July 26, 2000

Pilar reached over me at 5:30 AM to turn off the alarm. For a change, she had to wake up earlier than me today so she could catch a flight to Baltimore. Eddie's body arrived from Scotland yesterday, and his family scheduled the memorial service today. Pilar needed to get there earlier so she could view his body and, in a way, say good-bye before his cremation.

I felt guilty not going—for Pilar's support as much as to pay my respects to Eddie—but I knew Pilar would be surrounded by loved ones. She and one of her best friends from Puerto Rico got cheap flights to Baltimore, where they would grab a rental and drive to Alexandria. I kissed her good-bye before hopping into the shower. As I stood under the hot water, I stared blankly at the wall. Eddie's death still didn't feel real to me.

Evan woke up hungry that morning. I plopped him down in his high chair for breakfast in front of the TV. The kids' show *Blues Clues* played, and Evan watched it intently while munching on a waffle. He had already seen this same episode a couple times, but that didn't seem to matter to him. While it drives most adults nuts to see the same stuff repeatedly, kids seem to lap it up. More to the point, they need that level of repetition to encode the information they absorb.

The writers of this show obviously know this, so they show the same show all week. They also pilot test each episode to ensure that they hold kids' attention for the entire program. Pilar and I would cope with the monotony by privately mocking the show's host, Steve or that saltshaker character with the bad French accent.

Back then, Evan loved that show so much we took him to Boston's Wang Theater to see a live production featuring all the characters. When Steve took the stage, Evan couldn't contain his excitement. He jumped up and yelled, "I see Steve!" Then he ran from his seat, down the aisle, and stormed the stage like a hysterical Beatles fan. I chased after him laughing the whole way.

The day at my office ran smoothly. A newspaper reporter called for a phone interview about a sport psychology-related subject. For maybe the fourth or fifth time, this guy wanted my take on why sports fans get so crazed about their team's ups and downs. Since nothing dramatic happened recently in the world of sports, I figured it must have been a slow news day. I fought the urge to blurt out, "You know, some fans can't stand looking at their own hollow existence, so they redirect their rage and helplessness at their hometown team!"

Over the years, I progressed from feeling excited about doing such interviews to tolerating them as a professional necessity. It's not that I don't like talking about the subject matter—far from it. But you find yourself answering the same old questions after a while (like it's the fourth time you've seen the same *Blues Clues* show). Plus, these deadline-driven reporters often expect that you drop what you're doing to take their calls. If they call again a couple of hours later, they often sound irate that you didn't respond right away to their time-sensitive queries.

In my last appointment of the day, one of my clients, a scientist by training, got me into this deep discussion about Stephen Hawking—the brilliant physicist whose work, among many other things, has shed light on the birth of our universe. The whole discussion initially began because of my client's interest in the big picture about why he worried so much about seemingly little issues—a very perplexing and uncomfortable subject for him to address. By exploring the many unknowns about the universe, we had shifted into his comfort zone.

At times, I like to indulge such fascinations with certain clients—much like the conversations I have with Joe about the gray areas within the martial arts (which he calls the fringe)—because it helps me to find a common interest and connection with them. Eventually, I find a way to reel us both in and segue over to more directly relevant concerns.

In the case of this client, I did this by sharing something Albert Einstein once said about our interconnectedness with all things in our universe. This pertained to my client's feelings of alienation from his family and coworkers. I read aloud the following passage, which I had stored along with other poignant quotations and writings in one of my office files:

> A human being is part of a whole, called by us "Universe", a part limited in time and space. He experiences himself, his thoughts and feelings as something separated from the rest—a kind of optical delusion of his consciousness. This delusion is a kind of prison for

us, restricting us to our personal desires and to affection for a few persons nearest to us. Our task must be to free ourselves from this prison by widening our circle of compassion to embrace all living creatures ... Nobody is able to achieve this completely, but the striving for such achievement is in itself a part of the liberation, and a foundation for inner security.

By sharing this particular insight, I reached out to my client with an important message for him that met him at his level. Another person may have responded better to a Zen parable, biblical passage, or a poem by Robert Frost. The science behind Einstein's perspective—and his challenge to all of us—carried a stronger appeal to my client. Thankfully, it did seem to ease his sense of disconnection. And it offered a new viewpoint from which he could resume his efforts to relate more comfortably with others.

Now, I'd be lying if I said that such deep conversations don't touch *me* in a positive way as well. Despite my typical upbeat demeanor, I'm not immune to the drain of life's daily hassles. A big-picture perspective often reminds me of the relative triviality and transience of my concerns—which usually relieves me at least momentarily of my existential angst.

I was done at the office early because I had a follow-up appointment with my physician to check on my lungs. A nurse led me to an exam room where I would await my doctor. She pulled a wisp of a curtain in front of an exam table, handed me a johnny, and told me I should take off my shirt behind the curtain and that I could put on the johnny if I preferred. I couldn't help but smirk at the modesty implied by her gestures. *It's not like the doc hasn't already rummaged around my private areas before,* I wanted to say, *so you think I'm worried about her seeing me with my shirt off?* I kept my thoughts to myself and stepped behind the curtain.

Although she didn't think I had pneumonia, my doctor didn't like the way my breathing sounded through her stethoscope. She also didn't like the fact that the albuterol inhaler she previously gave me hadn't already cleared up the inflammation in my bronchial tubes. "Time for a steroid," she said pensively and then taught me how to use my second inhaler.

"What is this, Doc? And why isn't it going away?" I asked, genuinely perplexed, "I'm in a crucial stage of training to earn my black belt in karate—this couldn't be happening at a worse time."

"It probably originated from a cold you contracted because your immune system has gotten so drained. Now that it has progressed to your lungs, it doesn't seem to want to go away. Let's keep a close eye on this, and we'll follow up after a week or so." She wished me luck and sent me to the front desk to make an appointment.

At 5:00 PM, I swung by Evan's day care to pick him up. He was playing in the director's office when I arrived. Apparently, he threw a fit in finger-painting class, and while being whisked off for a time-out, he shouted at the teacher, "You'll pay for this!" It took all the strength I could muster not to burst out laughing. I could only imagine the scene in my head of the melodrama that must have ensued.

Except it wasn't that funny, considering that outbursts like these had occurred too often. The director and I spoke at length about Evan's unusual struggles with transitions during the day. Since this seemed unalterable through their typical means of handling such matters, she recommended that we involve a specialist to observe Evan in action. I would later contact Dr. Kent, the first in a string of professionals who would come into our lives to help us understand Evan's social and behavioral challenges. It was Dr. Kent who would eventually recommend that we switch Evan to a child-care program that could better accommodate his needs.

We headed home to find our baby sitter parked in front of our house, reading in her car. My unexpected meeting with Evan's school director forced me to run late, but she seemed not to mind. A tireless worker, Francesca attended high school during days and waited tables nightly at her family's restaurant (named after her by her father, Gerardo, an Italian immigrant and talented chef).

We first met her when she took our order the first time we dined at Francesca's. She was eleven years old but very comfortable bantering with customers, and we liked her immediately. Now, she was about to graduate high school, and I leaned on her heavily throughout this test for her help in watching Evan during her spare time. A few times, we actually had to get special permission from her to dad to spring her from the restaurant so she could help me with Evan. Joe's karate school sits across the street from his place, so we played the sentimental angle a bit to get him to concede.

I arrived at the dojo about a half hour before showtime that evening. The mood among my comrades seemed reasonably light, probably because of our good performance the night before. Despite a few sore spots on my body, the shoulder seemed okay, and my legs felt nice and loose.

Joe would later say he considered this our best night of Hell Week. But if I went strictly on gut feeling, I would've deemed it my worst. Personally, I felt off balance a good part of the night. Where Tuesday night contained mostly straightforward martial techniques, Wednesday night seemed like an entirely different ballgame. Like Red Sox ace Pedro Martinez, Joe had loosened us up with some straight-ahead heaters, and now it was time for his curveballs and changeups.

Even then, I knew this was Joe's way to take us into the fringe of our martial repertoires. He wanted to push us beyond the safety of the familiar. He started us off by instructing us to make up a brand-new kata on the spot—the equivalent of improvisational theater—and then had us reproduce it throughout the evening. Unlike my earlier creation entitled, "I Ching Kick-Line Kata," which I had many days to develop and can remember in exquisite detail, to this day, I cannot recall whatever I came up with that night.

After moving away from our new forms, we began stop-kata drills, requiring our minds to shift seamlessly from one form into others containing a common link. For example, Joe stopped us in the middle of Statue of the Crane, at the point where you deliver a simultaneous left upward arm block and a right poke to the opponent's throat. He then told us to shift to the exact same block strike occurring in another form (four kata) and then to complete that form.

Those were the easy ones, the techniques that only happen in one or two other forms. Even if you blanked out or became unsure, you could use your peripheral vision and see if your comrades made the same choice you did. And if for some reason you missed it, you could see the right choice and shift quickly over to recover. Joe knows this, of course, so he added two twists as the drill progressed.

The first thing he did was to stop our forms at places where the technique appears in several forms—thus creating many possible right answers. This made it harder to instantly check among your peers to see if you selected wisely, because we all could have shifted correctly over to different forms. In that case, checking your neighbor's movements would offer little help if you got lost.

The second curveball Joe threw at us came later when he had us close our eyes. This eliminates reference points such as your comrades' movements and the various angles in the dojo you can associate with specific parts of a kata (which you can recall from pure rote memory after doing them countless times in that room). That leaves only the sense of sound—critical for avoiding a crash into others doing their forms—and your muscle memory for executing proper turning angles within a specific kata.

Although I didn't smack into anybody during those segments of the test, I felt rather disoriented. And while we couldn't see ourselves, I'm sure we looked more like Iraqis in a fire drill than a well-trained group of martial artists.

On to combinations, punch techniques, weapons, and jujitsu techniques. Grand Master Ed Parker's Kenpo karate system includes a blend of elements drawn from other martial arts styles to amply prepare us for a variety of dangerous situations. So while karate is an unarmed martial art, practitioners learn how to handle attackers bearing knives, clubs, staffs, and, of course, guns. Our training includes what to do if the opponent is approaching or already in close range.

Joe had us do our techniques from every possible stance and angle. Our partners were told to try and confuse us about what kind of strike they would throw in our direction. This required us to rely on our well-developed instincts—to avoid preplanned defense strategies and quickly read the movements of our attackers. The type of technique we needed to use depended on whatever they threw at us. In that sense, we had to apply our system to real-life circumstances.

I wish I could say I passed this part with flying colors. I didn't. At one point, I couldn't get a technique to work, so I had to repeat it many times until I got it right. I entertained the thought that Joe might actually get as frustrated as me and dismiss me from the test. Naturally, this thought did nothing but distract my focus on the task at hand.

Somehow, though, we all made it through the confusing labyrinth that Joe placed us in. When he bowed us out and told us to report back at 8:00 PM the next night, I walked out dehydrated and in a daze.

It was late, probably 11:30 PM or so, and I recall all of us shaking our heads in disbelief as we quickly changed in the locker room. Since Joe ordered us to clear out of the dojo fast, we all agreed to meet and talk about the evening at the all-night laundromat next-door.

Usually the picture of composure and self-confidence, even Steven seemed shaken by the night's events. As we sat there sucking down fluids, we each shared our worst moments of the night and had a good laugh about it all—a much-needed comic relief. We also tried to guess at what Joe had looked for throughout the various drills we undertook. I think we all finally agreed that his exercises and methods seemed specifically *designed* to throw us off.

"I hope so," I chuckled, "because it worked. I was a mess out there."

So Joe had succeeded in taking us into the fringe of our martial arts knowledge. It's funny how you can feel like you know so much and, then in an instant, bow humbly to the realization of how much you don't know. We were the high-school senior hotshot know-it-alls of Joe's school at that time. Everyone else at the dojo, except the black belts of course, looked up to us as the rising stars. That night felt like our first taste of college, an introduction to the vastness of what we still had to learn.

After emptying our jugs of water and Gatorade, we adjourned our impromptu meeting and headed back to our homes. Two more days to go.

Chapter 27

Dan Gets the Key

Thursday, July 27, 2000

After arriving home around midnight, I paid a sleepy Francesca and thanked her profusely for pulling the longest babysitting shift of the past sixteen weeks. Ordinarily, Pilar would have relieved her by 8:30 PM or so, but Pilar hadn't yet returned from attending Eddie's funeral.

Stepping out of a quick shower, I noticed the message light flashing on our answering machine. Pilar called in to let me know how the funeral went. In a tired but surprisingly upbeat voice, she said she was okay—that many friends, family, and coworkers shared some great memories of Eddie at his funeral service.

When Pilar called, she and some close friends apparently were sipping wine in their hotel room, recalling the funny stuff Eddie used to say. She told me later that they laughed and cried until 3:00 AM or 4:00 AM, eventually succumbing to the exhaustion of their sad day together.

I had no appointments scheduled at the office until noon, so I slept in until Evan awoke around 7:00 AM. Squinting from the morning sunlight, I staggered into his room and pulled him from his crib. We hung out and ate breakfast together while watching yet another replay of *Blues Clues*.

I dropped Evan off midmorning at day care and headed over to the office. Pilar's plane would arrive that afternoon, and she planned to pick Evan up so I could drive directly to the dojo from work. She sounded understandably groggy on the phone but ready to come home.

My client appointments that day screamed diversity: an equestrian, a retired schoolteacher, an insurance adjuster, a college student, a small-company executive team, an ace software engineer, and a wealthy widow.

Many times, clients will jokingly ask how I keep from getting everybody's situations confused. Truthfully, I sometimes wonder myself how I can shift gears on the fly and tune into the next client's story.

In fact, that's what I tell them: that everyone has their story. Their life contains all the drama of a unique tale that gets written as we share time together. Each meeting we have offers me a little more of the story; then I must put the book away at session's end. I pick the book up the next time we meet, and I can usually jump right in where I left off with them. For those times where I need a little help with this (the client often forgets more than me), a quick glance at my notes, and, *snap,* I'm there.

At 7:15 PM, I left the office en route to Esposito's. Anticipating that the next eighteen hours would consist mainly of karate, I cleared my Friday calendar. On the way over to the dojo, I spoke briefly on my cell phone to Pilar. She had arrived safely and planned to crash early with Evan—still wiped out from her exhausting trip to DC.

Pilar wished me luck before I hung up, and I tried to turn my attention back to all things karate. Memories of the previous night's mental undressing during the test sent jolts of nervous energy through my body.

The gang sat there in a circle on the floor while I hurried through the lower dojo. They all looked over and nodded at me before I ducked into the locker room to change. Joining them on the floor, I remember the overriding sentiment in the group went something like, "Hey, whatever happens next, it'll all be over tomorrow afternoon." Somehow, resigning ourselves to whatever fate had in store for us seemed strangely comforting.

From our isolated hamlet downstairs, we could hear the kiais and the rumble of bodies hitting the floor from the class going on in the upper dojo. Our conversation wandered into the subject of what would happen after successfully completing this last night of Hell Week.

Barring any total meltdowns, we had to show up the following morning at five thirty by ourselves to prepare for our final day. And of course, Joe would present us with the question of who would take responsibility for opening up the dojo. That person would naturally have to hold on to the *key* and return it to Joe afterward. A simple task for sure but laced with superstition following that whole key debacle which occurred a couple years earlier.

Danny Walsh volunteered. He's a cop, a straight arrow, and as dependable as the earth's gravity. Plus, at that time, he lived right next-door to the dojo. How could he lose the damn key between Joe's office and his mom's house not fifty feet away? Yep, if we made it through that night, we all agreed, Dan gets the key.

This concern about losing the dojo key reminded me of an old Persian parable I like to share with clients. As the story goes, a young man searched in vain for his key outside his home. One of his neighbors, upon hearing of this man's problem, offered to help. After a fruitless period of time, the neighbor suggested that the man try to recall the last time he saw the key. To this, the man replied that he thought he might have seen it last inside his house.

Understandably frustrated, the neighbor asked, "If you think the key is inside, why do you look for it outside?" The young man thought for a moment and then said, "Well, because it's lighter out here."

Beyond the obvious contempt we may have for the young man in this story, we must not judge him too quickly. He searches for something important, in this case, a key. He clearly needs to look inside his house, a metaphor for his inner self—perhaps a darker, scarier place to examine. Instead, he tries taking the easier path of finding the answers he seeks (i.e., the key) outside himself.

This happens more often than you think. People tend to blame others for their unhappiness. Yet the longer they fixate on factors beyond their control, the more angry and helpless they feel. This parable suggests that we instead focus on the things we can control—how we *react* to life's challenges. In effect, the *key* to addressing our problems lies literally *inside* us.

We heard the pounding footsteps and laughter of sweat-drenched students coming downstairs toward the locker rooms. This meant that we would soon get the call to go upstairs and line up for our final night of Hell Week. That call came at 8:15.

We bowed ourselves into a steamy dojo—complete with the mirrors fogged up from the class before. Having taken so many of Joe's intense Thursday-night classes before, the sweaty smell hanging in the humid air didn't surprise me. But tonight, something else felt different. Something smelled different.

Even though the class had cleared out fifteen minutes earlier, and the door remained open, the room still seemed too warm. Sure, it was midsummer, but the temperature had dropped into the sixties by nightfall. So we couldn't blame the weather. Within minutes, my skin went from moist—caused by my earlier warm-up—to dripping, and we hadn't even begun our night.

Then it dawned on me: Joe had turned the heat on. I knew it—that smell, that faint scent of dusty oil heat pumping out of the dojo wall vents. With or without Mother Nature's help, Joe wanted to make sure that heat would remain a factor throughout that night.

From the opening bell, Joe had us come out swinging with high-intensity basic drills. In an effort to rise to Joe's challenge, we screamed our kiais in unison. Our eyes focused dead ahead on imaginary opponents. Before each piercing kiai, you could hear our gis snap with the crispness of our movements. I could feel my heart and lungs scramble to keep up with my body's urgent demand for fresh oxygen.

Where overthinking became my primary distraction the night before, heat and fatigue would accompany my thoughts throughout Thursday night's test. I recall frequently sensing my tired limbs and panting lungs, but then shifting swiftly back to the techniques at hand. "Center your breath," I would remind myself, "you'll recover during the breaks and seams (momentary lapses in the action, such as the brief times between forms or other drills)."

Besides my own internal reminders of my fatigue, I could see the various indicators of distress in my comrades as well. At one point, I noticed Dan sweating profusely. During a particularly intense drill involving flips and throws onto a blue vinyl crash mat, Dan popped up and stood on the mat, ready to go again.

As I faced Dan, something caught my eye down on the mat: a rapidly growing puddle of clear liquid spreading outward from his feet. He literally had streams of sweat running down the pant creases of his saturated gi.

While the night bore on, all of us started to fade. You could tell by the drooping stances, softer kiais, and ragged techniques—this, despite two breaks where Joe sent us downstairs to rehydrate and recover mentally and physically.

The sport psychologist in me wishes I could say I made a conscious decision to do what I did next. It happened more out of pragmatic necessity. Like the situation called upon me to react a certain way, and that's what happened. All night long, I fought through a mental gauntlet, forcing me to deflect and subdue all my distractions—they represented my opponents just as much as the guys or Joe or anybody else—those pesky little hobgoblins of doubt that can weigh you down. Then probably out of sheer exhaustion, I just let them all go.

Letting go of all concerns about collapsing, hurting my shoulder or someone else, coughing my lungs out, or flunking the test made me feel freer, lighter. I knew something special happened when I went to throw a flying side-blade kick during one of our forms. That's the cool-looking kick you often see in martial arts ads or magazines. The real pros fly over big objects and other people en route to breaking someone in half with the kick itself.

Since I ordinarily have little elevation with all my aerial kicks, I don't really *fly* during my flying side-blade kick; it looks more like I'm hopping. Once again, this doesn't hurt me from a standpoint of hitting a higher target because of my height. The problem would come if I ever needed to clear something or someone bigger than a midget. In such cases, my typical hop kick wouldn't do. But this time, I swear I actually *flew*. It was an exhilarating feeling that served to inspire me down the homestretch.

Throughout the inner battle I fought that night, one centering thought or belief helped to neutralize the doubts that clamored for my attention: trust. Sounds too simple, but it proved a powerful defense against all the garbage that littered my mental landscape. "Trust your skills and your conditioning," I reminded myself over and over, "they'll carry you through this." And they did just that.

Finally, around midnight, Joe had us assemble in our standing pattern of four. We bowed, meditated, and then Joe reviewed with us the details of what he expected of us the following morning. And when he posed the question as to whom we would entrust with the dojo key, we all pointed to Dan.

That was it—we made it to Friday. One more day to go.

Chapter 28

Commencement Day

You always hear at graduation ceremonies someone referring to the dual meaning of the word "commencement"—signifying the end of one journey and the beginning of another. For the rest of my life, I will always regard Friday, July 28, 2000, as one of those landmark days.

After showering and winding down a bit, I didn't fall asleep that morning until around 1:30. Not good, given that I had to set my alarm for 4:30 so I could eat and get to the dojo by 5:30. Dave would later tell me he only managed to sleep about an hour because of his Thursday-night adrenaline hangover.

Still mostly asleep, Pilar wished me a muffled, "Good luck," through her pillow as I packed my gear. Before stepping out the door into the predawn light, I stuffed a few large bottles of Gatorade into my bag. As I filled my tired lungs with the cool morning air, they ached a little like the way they used to feel after swimming all day as a kid.

The temperature hadn't climbed above the seventies all week long, and today also promised to be another unusually cool day for July in the Boston area. In retrospect, this seems fitting, because our first pretest took place on that snowy, rainy, cool day the prior April.

On the ride over to Joe's, I cranked a high-energy collection of music on my cassette deck. I selected this tape specifically to psych myself up before every test during Hell Week. While listening to these tunes, my mind would drift to brief imagery sequences of myself performing well during the test that day. As I turned on to Adams Street toward Esposito's, the old Saga song "Wind Him Up" came on. *Perfect,* I grinned to myself.

Steve and Dan sat outside waiting for Dave and me to show up. Dan smirked as he waved the dojo key, which meant we would all have the opportunity to cross the finish line that day. I smiled and waved back from my car, acknowledging perhaps the ridiculousness of our concern over remembering a stupid key. Dave pulled in right behind me, and we went in to set up shop.

As tired as we felt, a buzz of energy hummed within us like the overhead fluorescent lights in the downstairs area. With not much to review at this point, we didn't say a lot to each other—only an occasional word of encouragement.

About 5:50 AM, we headed upstairs to the dojo to wait for Joe. We knew he had entered the building because we heard the heat go on. Joe always hates the cold, but it was July, and we knew from last night that this was for our dubious benefit. He wanted the dojo to get toasty again for us.

I had lost track of the time, and Joe walked in exactly at 6:00 AM—just after I wondered aloud to the guys why I had not received a solid shot to my gut from any of the black belts yet. Getting punched or kicked in the abdominals occurs occasionally during training and tests to ensure that you always stay prepared during an actual fight to receive a painful strike. Joe slammed the door shut and pretty much finished my sentence with a curt directive for us to line up in formation. My mouth dropped open.

No way—that didn't just happen, I thought to myself in disbelief as I rushed over to my spot, *what an idiot!*

I knew Joe heard me, and the question remained as to what he might choose to do about it. Either way, I didn't have the luxury to worry about it for long. I had to redirect my focus back to his next instructions.

For the first time in sixteen weeks, Joe served as the only black belt witness. Seven green folding chairs sat empty at the front of the dojo. After bowing us in and having us meditate a moment, Joe took a seat in the middle chair and got us started.

An awareness of the importance of that moment provided more than enough charge to turn over our tired engines. As usual, we began our adrenaline surge with hard and fast basics. Our early-morning voices cleared with every kiai, and our reluctant muscles obeyed the call to action. Once again, the heat quickly brought our body temperatures up, and the sweat started to flow.

After an extended warm-up with basics, Joe had me, Dan and Dave assume training stances facing the right wall—with only our feet and knees touching the off-white sheetrock surface. Steven stayed at attention in the middle of the room. Joe directed him to perform several katas, some repeatedly, while he assessed every nuance.

We just held our training stances and stared straight into the wall while awaiting our turns. I listened to Steven's movements. Without intention, I started following in my head his progression through every kata—except his own form, because I hadn't encoded its content. Eventually, it crossed my mind that Joe might actually expect us to identify Steven's stance or technique at any given point, so I continued mentally tracing everyone's steps while I awaited my turn. And as I did this, sweat drops slowly tickled my face as they meandered downward from my scalp and forehead.

After Dave's turn in the spotlight, Joe called us all out to join him on the floor. We did each other's best and worst katas—the ones Joe had previously asked us to identify. When we got to my worst, Statue of the Crane, Joe stopped us right as we landed our third crane stance.

This left us facing the flag wall, balancing on the left foot while holding the right leg up—knee bent—to the point where the thigh stayed parallel to the floor. While our shoulders and hips stood square to the flag wall, our heads faced right toward the mirrors. This enabled us to stare at ourselves standing there frozen in our stances. Ironically, Joe had made us transform literally into statues of cranes.

After a moment, Joe actually left the dojo! He told us to hold our stances until he returned—but he warned us not to let our right foot touch the floor and that he had better not walk back in to find any of us out of position. *Well, that's just great,* I thought as Joe shut the door.

Dan muttered under his breath some kind of grievance with my choosing this kata—like I could have somehow anticipated Joe would concoct this specific form of torture. I just softly chuckled and said, "Sorry, guys."

So there we stood, wobbling on one foot for what seemed like an eternity. The time frame before Joe returned to the room probably lasted more like ten minutes. But when your right hip flexor and thigh muscles burn intensely in a bath of lactic acid, ten minutes can seem a lot longer.

I wish I could say that I doggedly held that stoic stance for the entire time. I will confess that I did shake my leg out a couple times to bring the circulation back into my right leg. And though my right foot never touched ground, it may have found my left knee before Joe came storming back into the dojo. Before he even closed the door, he said simply, "Okay, continue your form."

Now, I know we all remembered the kata we had begun awhile earlier. Unfortunately, one or two of us apparently forgot which crane stance we left off on before our little statue drill. Of course, this prompted Joe to stop and have us start again from the proper place in the kata. Except he stopped us again after the next three strikes even though I think we all got it right this time.

Joe then proceeded to instruct us to repeat the same three-strike sequence and called out the number 1 when we finished. Then we did it again, yelling, "Two," at the end. And we kept on doing the same sequence until we reached one hundred.

If the saying "Repetition is the mother of all learning" is true, then we must have learned one mother of a lesson that day. I know for me at least, I don't consider Statue of the Crane my worst form anymore.

After the crane saga drew to a close, Joe gave us a water break—but this time we had to stay in the dojo, the first time all week. *Different,* I thought, *but no biggie*. I had left my Gatorade bottles in my gym bag. Unknown to the rest of us at the time, though, Dan had apparently stashed a gallon of water downstairs, where he fully expected to have access to it during our first break. All he had with him was a one-liter bottle, which he would have to ration. Given Dan's ability to sweat, this represented a serious problem.

When we resumed action, Joe stuck with the kata theme. One challenging drill involved our performing a series of punch techniques taken from different forms. We would have to do these forms with the attacker coming from different directions, using various strikes—requiring us to quickly convert a rote skill into a mirror image of itself. Forced to "see" the attacker from a new perspective, we needed to react more out of instinct when the strike came.

That drill seemed to go okay until for some reason, I got spun around on a simple strike-block combination that occurs toward the end of five kata. Like an everyday word you inexplicably can't recall, I couldn't retrieve the proper footwork and kept facing the wrong way. In the spirit of "Do something—don't just stand there frozen," I continued doing it wrong with the hope that the correct pattern would mercifully reappear in my mind. It never did.

Without looking at Joe, I sensed that he was as perplexed as I was that I couldn't get back on track—no matter how many times he repeated the drill. Part worried, part frustrated, I must have done it eight or nine times before Joe thankfully moved on.

Shortly after that little meltdown, Joe called on us to kneel and meditate. As I breathlessly assumed our meditation position, I thought that this could not be the end; it was simply too early. Joe then told us to look up. He held a black belt in his hands and said that normally, at this point in the test, he would have us each hold the belt a moment. This would symbolize that the end of our journey was near.

Then after a brief pause, his tone sharpened, and he recanted, "But we're so f—g far from that right now that I'm not even gonna bother." With that said, he turned to his right and whipped the belt against the wall, and it thudded to the floor.

Our drills continued until Joe finally told us to take another water break. Unfortunately for Dan, this one also took place in the dojo itself. Dan sipped what little water had collected back on the bottom of his first bottle, and then he looked over at Steven. Steven had just pulled out a fresh new bottle and chugged most of it down, unaware of his comrade's wanting eyes. Dan would later quip, "I'd have slit my mother's throat for that water bottle," but instead of motioning for a sip, he kept his distress to himself.

Just as Joe lined us up into our starting pattern of four, several black belts entered the dojo. Among the new witnesses were Steven's father and stepmother. After they filled the remaining empty chairs, Joe said that they would now begin the official part of the test. And with that, he had us start again with basics.

It was 9:00 AM. We had already been at it for three hours, and we had only just begun "the official part" of the test. *What the f— do you call the first part?* I asked myself incredulously between kiais. *You know he's just testing our resolve,* I reminded myself as I tried to refocus on the task at hand.

After an extended basics drill where Joe had us calling out the strikes, we went though all our techniques—sometimes on each other, sometimes against imaginary opponents. When we moved on to the mats, I knew we had reached the crash-and-bash segment: these drills involved hard contact with each other and the floor. And Joe wanted us to air it all out for his other black belts. He wanted them to know that our technique and intensity would meet his gold standard for the rank.

At one point during these drills, I recall Greg Steelman, one of the more well-liked black belts, tell us to "Savor this moment, guys—'cause before you know it, it's gonna be all over." I know that he meant that as a way for us to not simply wish away our time in this test. That we should take some appreciation in the importance of what we were participating in at that moment. But by then, we had no room left in our weary hearts for such a nostalgic view of our situation—we wanted it to end and to end soon.

By noon that day, I personally felt drained of nearly everything I had in my gas tank. I began the day at 4:30 AM, and the test had run now for the past six hours. All the conditioning and training that helped carry me this far now seemed to fade into a blur of exhaustion. Between sets of techniques and katas, my legs shook as I struggled to maintain the low squat of my training stance and to catch my breath.

My cough, which had worsened gradually over the past two weeks, made it difficult for me to recover as quickly when we had less strenuous intervals. It felt like I imagine a team of bleary climbers must feel as they stumble their way to the summit of Mt. Everest.

My bare feet stung with the cumulative rug burn of the dojo's floor carpeting. Thousands of steps, drags, tumbles, and takedowns had brushed its surface each year, wearing the carpet down to a paper-thin flannel covering atop that concrete suspension floor. Steven would later say that his feet were fine but that the skin under his arms burned from the chafing from his sweat-drenched gi top.

I could smell that same putrid mix of body odor and dusty oil heat as it pumped through the aluminum wall vents and circulated the stale air. This, along with the poor condition of my lungs made me light-headed, but I clung to the sound of Joe's voice. Now more than at any other time in this test, the importance of his approval hung unmistakably in the forefront of everyone's consciousness.

Like a conditioned Pavlovian response, Joe's voice had become associated with the fear of disapproval and failure. It had the effect of triggering electrical surges through my body, followed by an unspoken eagerness to comply. By this blurry point in the test, I had actually grown to rely upon those energy bursts caused by his commands, as though Joe had actually become my adrenal glands. Like the night before, I had no choice but to let go of my fears and trust my mind and body to carry me through this challenge.

Then Joe had us face the flag wall, but this time we could stand upright at attention—instead of squatting down in a training stance. A sweet, merciful gesture, this helped preserve whatever strength we would need for what remained of the test. Nevertheless, I could barely keep from swaying in my position as Joe called us out one by one to read our essays to the black belts.

When Joe had me come out, he told the black belts to take special notice of what I had to say. He handed me my essay, and I noticed Steve Nugent nodding slightly just before I turned my eyes to the pages in my hands. My hands and voice quivered initially, but then I straightened up and yelled out hoarsely while reading the document.

Not long after Dave read his essay, Joe finally told my fellow students and I to come off the wall, kneel, and begin meditation. I felt my spent body gratefully succumb to the gravitational pull toward the welcoming floor. *We made it—the test was over,* I so desperately hoped in my mind.

Or was it? I wondered, my mind still not ready to let my guard down completely. At that point, it would not have surprised me if Joe did this to see if we could summon whatever energy we had left to engage in some other task. *This feels so good,* I thought, *but this isn't over 'til it's over,* trying to ready myself for the command to get up and assume a fighting stance.

My forehead rested on the floor in the space between my hands—which faced downward in the triangular, I Ching position, the symbolic component I wove into the kata I designed during this test. This everyday gesture we practice in all classes felt so appropriate—if not poetic—for that moment: to reflect on the Chinese book of changes after all of the changes we had personally undergone in the past sixteen weeks.

Between brief coughing spells, I pulled the air back into my tired lungs in long, slow breaths. Each time I exhaled, I let my body melt a little more into the floor, as I let go of all unnecessary tension in my body. My mind focused on a place just below my navel, the center of my breath—my one point—the very same location where my body's center of gravity rested. In and out of the dojo, this centering technique has faithfully served as my refuge for collecting my thoughts during many pressure situations. As I described earlier, it literally carried me through this test up until this point.

While maintaining my meditative position, I could hear the black belts laying our belts in front of us. *Yes!* I said to myself, *we did it!*

I knelt third in a row of four as Joe and the other black belts in attendance awarded us our black belt one by one. As it started to sink in that I had achieved—that we had achieved—this new rank, I sobbed quietly into the floor. It was like letting go of my defenses, my attitude—the hard edge that I had to maintain for so long.

Perhaps the most emotional one in the room at that time, though, was Rob Leckie: his eighteen-year-old son had just made it through Hell Week, the youngest of Joe's students ever to do this. His voice cracked slightly as Joe had him personally award Steven his black belt.

We all felt exhausted yet exhilarated. We had reached the summit of our climb up Everest. We embraced and took our photos not with the Himalayas in the background but instead with the American flag that a fellow student had once painted on the dojo wall. Then we all went out for a late lunch to take in the view from the top of the world. All except Dan, who went home to crash.

As we nibbled on appetizers and rehydrated slowly, Steven, Dave, and I sat around a table with Joe and the other black belts recounting the events of that morning. His game face long gone, Joe praised us repeatedly for a job well done. I recall sitting there uncharacteristically quiet, still in awe of what we had accomplished. You could almost see it on my face in the photos someone took of us that day in the restaurant.

A couple hours later, I left the restaurant to pick up my son at day care. The test was finally over. Evan matter-of-factly gave me a toy to hold as he walked out with me to the car. Funny, I had just come home from an intense personal journey, and he had no clue about the enormity of what just happened to me.

The great basketball coach John Wooden once said that after winning his first national championship, a pigeon pooped on his head as he walked out of his hotel room. In true Wooden fashion, he just laughed with his wife and took this to mean that he must not be that important after all.

I guess the message is to not lose perspective on the experience. I didn't solve the riddle of AIDS or cancer, nor did I negotiate a peace agreement in the Middle East. The only thing I did was, as in the parable of the black belt, to begin my never-ending journey of self-improvement through discipline.

Evan wouldn't get it that day—nobody could, regardless of their age, except for those who've been through something similar. That's probably why I wrote about this journey: so he would one day understand what I did when he was nearly three years old and perhaps that he might someday take up his own path toward personal excellence.

My uncle: Lt. George Young, 5th Infantry, WWII

My parents: Bob and Diane Smith in Newport, R.I.

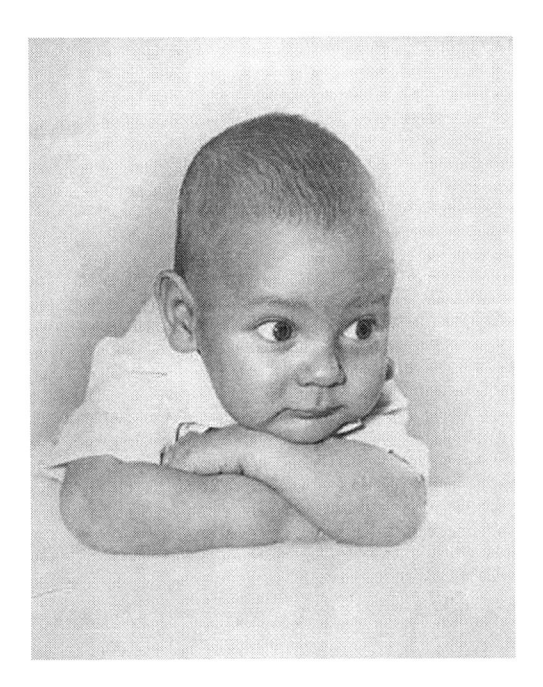

My infamous "Meatball" photo, taken in 1961

From Meatball to 4th National Prize winner in photo contest

Goofing around with my kid brother, Joey at a trade show

Prom shot sporting that Keith Partridge-Willy Wonka look
(I paid Joey to join me)

Sound of Music: encore bow with my talented co-star

Tip-off at state tourney with my East Catholic teammates

Me dunking at NMH—back when I had some springs

Friend and mentor Dr. Dan Kirschenbaum
after doing the "Rocky" run with me in Philadelphia

Mom, Dad, Kim and I pose with Joe at his graduation

My sister Kim and her newlywed husband, Brian, 1985

Joe poses with me in my first major purchase
after getting my Ph.D. in 1988

My wife Pilar, on a hike near Kent Falls in CT

Iglesia San Jose, Old San Juan, Puerto Rico: the 500 year old church where Pilar and I got married in 1990

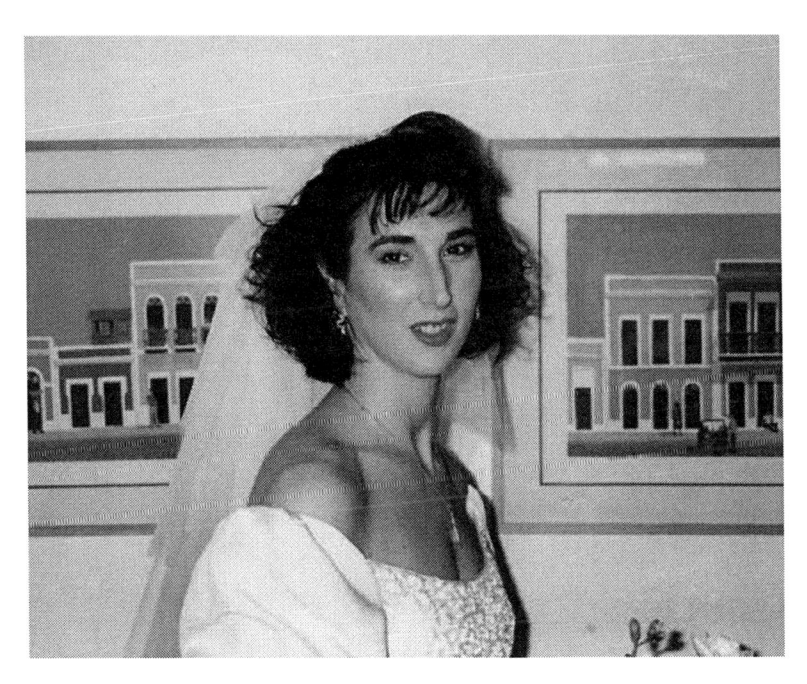

Pilar looks stunning during her prep for our wedding

Pilar and I march triumphantly down the aisle:
definitely one of the best days of my life

Getting a stretch from a friend at East Coast
Tae Kwon Do in Bridgeport, CT

Me sparring at a local Tae Kwon Do tourney,
I think they gave me the point on that one

From East Coast Tae Kwon Do, Bridgeport, CT: are (back row, L-R) Gus Vlamis, Master Ed Mezerewski, and Billy Petrone (5-time national champ and former U.S. National Tae Kwon Do Team member); In front: Colby Mezerewski, Casey Mezerewski, and Derek Person

Grand Master Esposito's flying side blade kick over the head of his friend and black belt student, Dan Donovan

Me posing with Evan on his 1st Halloween

Col. Arnold Scheller, M.D., and Capt. Glen Ross, M.D. enjoying a
ProSports function in Waltham, MA

Woody (Don Worden): an ace physical therapist
and all-around good guy

My black belt comrades and I pose with Grand Master Esposito at a reunion dinner: Steven, Dan Joe, Dave, and Me

Pilar and I enjoying the food and the view from Asolare's deck in St. John, USVI, where we celebrated our 10th wedding anniversary

The one and only Eddie Diaz, 1959-2000

Steven poses proudly with his dad, Dr. Rob Leckie
after receiving his father's black belt, July 28, 2000

Grand Master Esposito with Dan after he received his black belt on July 28, 2000

A dynamic duo as karate instructors, Joe and Cathy Esposito pose before their school logo in their main dojo, Newton, MA

Me posing in Waltham, MA in full uniform

Evan—the next generation—hits a fighting stance
as a white belt in 2005

Chapter 29

Returning To Civilization: The Descent

Since you can never linger too long at the summit of any achievement, I inevitably had to begin my downward descent toward the base of the mountain—otherwise known as my life outside of karate. Much of my home and work commitments had circled in a virtual holding pattern during the test, especially the last month. I had a sport psychology chapter to complete with a colleague for an impatient book publisher. Clients needed more evening-hour appointment openings. My son needed me to stop hurriedly shuffling him off to babysitters after day care so I could make it to karate classes. My wife needed more of my undivided love and attention.

In the first few days after July 28, I felt myself coming down from the exhilarating high of this intense experience. I needed a break to recuperate and begin processing what had just happened, but in my mind, I had no time for that. We celebrated Evan's third birthday the following Monday. So, of course, that meant a mad scramble over the weekend just to get the house ready for his party. Per Evan's special request, we went for a tasteful *Teletubbies* theme, and all seemed to go well.

On Tuesday, I had to report to jury duty. Of the many times I have received a summons to serve previously, this time they actually made me sit through a trial. In this case, some moron left a pile of marijuana on his kitchen table, and his girlfriend let a cop in to discuss another matter. While I didn't necessarily want the guy to walk, the cop apparently failed to show just cause for searching the apartment, so the judge let him go on that technicality. Didn't that cop ever watch TV's *Law & Order?* As an assistant DA, Sam Waterson's character cuts suspects loose every week for stuff like that. In any case, this cop's oversight helped get me dismissed early, so I could go back and clean up my desk at the office.

164

The following night—I'm not kidding—we had tickets to see Carlos Santana play at the Tweeter Center, a Boston-area outdoor concert venue. We tailgated and had a great time at the show. Santana played his best stuff—the guy hasn't aged a bit.

It didn't take long after that week for me to crash—mainly in the form of physical illness and exhaustion. From April to July, Joe Esposito had tweaked our conditioning to levels beyond my imagination. But by mid-August, I felt my body breaking down.

I had forgotten a cardinal rule of training in the martial arts: a seeming oxymoron called disciplined rest. Contrary to today's popular notion that "more is better," even ancient warriors knew that our minds and bodies needed regular intervals of rest to maximize the benefits of conditioning. Unknowingly, I was about to learn firsthand about the dangers of not heeding this training tenet.

My cough worsened to the point where I couldn't breathe at night when lying flat in bed. My lungs fell into a spiral of constantly filling up with fluid, only to have progressively more difficulty expelling the phlegm because the excessive coughing had irritated my already swollen bronchial airways. My struggle for air reminded me of when I nearly drowned at Spring Pond as a nine-year-old.

After another visit to my doctor's office, my diagnosis finally became clear: I had something called exercise-induced asthma. It turned out that this episode would take me months to overcome.

Ironically, my comparing the black belt test to climbing a mountain would also include the recovery from such feats—most noticeably in my case with the onset of my illness and asthma episode. Apparently, a physical breakdown often follows an extremely demanding expedition with many elite mountain climbers.

Experts at the U.S. Olympic Training Center say that athletes training at high altitudes must function with approximately one-third less oxygen than at sea level. Try breathing half breaths for a little while, and you'll get an idea of what that might feel like.

To avoid cramping and exhaustion, high-altitude alpinists need to consume greater amounts of liquids and carbohydrates, and they must constantly watch for signs of altitude sickness and asthma as they reach ever-higher elevations. Also, these extreme conditions suppress the immune system, which makes them more vulnerable to infections.

During the black belt test, my frequent bouts with cramps no doubt came because I didn't properly guard against dehydration. And my cough had probably started as a cold—contracted during the summer, no less—and it got worse in July as my immune system became exhausted. The enormous drain of Hell Week, coupled with my lack of rest afterward, probably caused my cough to progress into asthma.

Despite my stubborn adherence to my work and family obligations, I did slow down and eventually recovered. But initially because of my lack of energy, I never returned to Esposito's to attend class as the other guys did—nor did I stop by to say hi to the old gang. And although I have continued to stay in contact with Joe and my test comrades, it would be four years before I set foot in the dojo again for a class.

Between my extended recuperation period and the burnout inherent in the process of eating and sleeping karate for so long, the other priorities in my life slipped back ahead of the martial arts. Office appointments with clients took the place of my evening karate classes. I finished that sport psychology book chapter. And Evan got his daddy back.

Over the months that followed, Dave or Steve would occasionally give me some crap about not returning to class. They would point to all the neat new techniques they had learned in Joe's exclusive black belt class—to which I would now be entitled to attend—and how much I would enjoy learning them. Each time, all I could do was shrug my shoulders in agreement and then say that I had other obligations but that I would return someday.

In the meantime, I never stopped practicing all the techniques and katas I have ever learned, including the form I'd created myself for the test. Since my office sits in the middle of a fitness center, I have had the freedom and facilities to stay in good physical condition and to keep my martial skills sharp. Perhaps somewhere in the back of my mind, I viewed my training as preparation for my return to Esposito's as one of his black belts: to continue my never-ending journey of self-improvement through discipline.

Rosie Torres, the widow of our good friend Eddie who died the Wednesday before Hell Week, has had more than her share of fights since July of 2000. In the following spring, she noticed a stranger heading briskly toward her front door while she weeded the lawn of her home.

With her daughter Victoria sleeping inside, Rosie instinctively raced to block his path. The man pulled out a knife, and in the struggle, she managed to fight him off, and he ran away but not before he had stabbed her seven times. She ran next-door covered in blood, and her neighbor called the police. They later found the man, and Rosie's testimony led to his conviction for aggravated assault.

Not even a year later, Rosie learned that she had breast cancer. After surgery and treatment, she went back to work and to raise her daughter.

As for my comrades that accompanied me on that journey in 2000, I never stop thinking about them. We stay in touch and see each other two or three times per year—especially around July to reconnect and reminisce. While we previously had little else in common other than karate, we all share a strong bond of mutual respect and admiration that sprung forth out of our experiences during Joe's black belt test. We are like old war buddies forever joined by those experiences.

In 2001, a test of that bond came in the form of a scare we all experienced when Dan went to see a doctor about pain in his jaw area. An x-ray revealed that a tumor had grown along the bone and that he needed to have surgery right away. Dan had the tumor removed, and the biopsy showed that it was malignant. A fast healer, Dan thankfully recovered completely from this procedure. He continues his work as a cop and to attend and teach classes with Dave and the other black belts at Esposito's.

Steven went back to Harvard as a premed student the fall that followed our black belt test. Not surprisingly, Steven ripped through their program and graduated with high honors in 2003. He completed his M.D. at the prestigious University of Massachusetts medical school program in Worcester, and now is a resident in Orthopedics at the University of Pittsburgh Medical Center. Perhaps one day, he'll join his father on the medical staff at a top Boston area hospital. As for his karate, Steven still trains and attends classes when he can, and he goes easy on his old man whenever they spar.

Joe and Cathy Esposito continue teaching the next generation of martial artists at their Newton school—where they devote their sizeable talents and tireless energy in promoting all the valuable skills and lessons inherent in martial arts training. In January of 2006, Joe got promoted to tenth degree, earning the title of "Grand Master" within the Kenpo style.

Chapter 30

Life Lessons Learned So Far

I wrote this book assuming the risk of sounding presumptuous or narcissistic. After all, who writes a memoir at forty-something? Who would care about my whiny middle-class upbringing or my having taken a karate test? Indeed, I am not a famous person, nor have I accomplished anything particularly newsworthy.

This, of course, assumes that people read books only written by famous people—or those who have done something extraordinary. It was my hope, in fact, to write a book that more people could relate with because it came from the experiences of someone who has to sit in shitty seats at concerts and ballgames—just like they do. Hopefully, you recognized a bit of yourselves in my narrative and took something from my story.

Whatever special qualities I have do not come from my PhD or my black belt. They come primarily from the value I can add to the lives of those whom I encounter in my life's journey: my family, friends, coworkers, and clients. And with this book, I have the chance to touch the lives of people I'll probably never meet but may help nonetheless through my message of resilience and hope.

So throwing caution to the wind, in this chapter I decided to share some of the lessons I've taken from my life experiences thus far, as seen through the eyes of a forty-seven-year-old psychologist and martial artist. Given my middle age, and the certainty that I still have much to learn about life, perhaps you can consider this collection of insights as a "Greatest Lessons, Volume 1." And if I am so inclined and inspired at eighty-something to undertake another similar exploration, I will add a second volume.

Let me first clarify that this chapter by no means includes a comprehensive list of wisdom pearls. Nor should you take these as facts. Instead, they reflect some of the helpful discoveries that have served me well along my journey. In the spirit of conciseness and as a tribute to David Letterman, I limited the number to the "Top 10 Life Lessons Learned So Far" (hey, I need to save something for volume 2).

10. *The martial arts are a living language.*

> Latin has been called a dead language, despite the fact that it is deeply embedded in English and the so-called romance languages. It's a dead language because no new words and expressions have sprung from it in centuries.
>
> To me, the martial arts seem like a language that our mind and body learns through training. Once mastered, we need to keep practicing them so we don't lose our fluency in thought or action. In that modifications to the timeless fundamentals of the martial arts have continued over the years, we can fairly view them as a *living language*. For example, two popular styles in the United States—Ed Parker's kenpo karate and Bruce Lee's *Jeet Kune Do*—only emerged onto the scene less than forty years ago.
>
> People who speak many languages say that they find it easier to learn the next new language. The patterns of grammar and word construction often share similarities to other tongues, preventing them from having to start from scratch. The same can be said of the martial arts. My previous experience of learning tae kwon do in Connecticut most certainly helped me learn the kenpo system more quickly when I moved to Boston.
>
> Much like a person must keep practicing their language to keep their fluency, I need to stay on top of my martial training. In the years since my black belt test, I've practiced all my techniques and katas at the gym where my office is located at least once per week. In the back of my mind, I always prepare myself for the day I step back into a karate class—ready to handle whatever or whomever sensei throws at me.

9. *Hydration and rest are essential to training.*

> After seeing a player succumb to a leg cramp during a recently televised game, basketball commentator Bill Walton wondered aloud, "Doesn't anybody drink water anymore? I don't get why so many guys are having cramps." For me, his incredulous tone struck home as much as the simplicity of his message: drink more water, avoid cramps.
>
> Most muscle cramps can be avoided if you stay properly hydrated. And you can't wait to feel thirsty to signal the need for

more fluids—by then it's too late. You're already dehydrated and at risk of cramping up.

At several points during the black belt test, I experienced the painful consequences of failing to stay hydrated. Apparently, I didn't learn from my first severe bout with cramping during the Run, which occurred toward the beginning of the test. It had to happen again and again during Hell Week before I connected the muscle spasms with insufficient fluids in my system.

During my office visit that last week, I recall my doctor commenting on my blood pressure changing significantly when she took it while I lied down and again while standing. "You're dehydrated," she said matter-of-factly. She went on to explain that large variations in your blood pressure indicate depleted fluid levels in your body.

In general, our body functions best when we drink between six to eight glasses of water daily. That's under *normal* circumstances. But athletes place more extreme demands on their body's circulatory and cooling systems. Obviously, they need to drink more than eight glasses during training to keep their high-performance engines running well. Like a race car, they must continually top off the engine's fluids to avoid problems associated with overheating on the road (or the field, court, or dojo).

I had asked my body to do more with less, and it let me know in no uncertain terms that it was not pleased. I finally listened during Hell Week.

Unfortunately, after Hell Week, my body once again clobbered me for not listening. This time, I failed to let it heal and rest before resuming my crazy work and personal life. My body's immune system broke down, and I dragged my tired body and lungs around for many weeks before things cleared up.

The Protestant work ethic notwithstanding—and I'm not even Protestant!—rest is *not* a four-letter word for candy asses. It's as critical to training as any workout or nutritional regimen.

This concept applies to life outside of physical training as well. Time and again, I am reminded—often by my wife—to put some boundaries around my work. If unchecked in my earlier years here in Boston, I would have worked seven days per week. This left little time for sleep, family, and a social life. Going full tilt, my body weight dropped from 215 to 200 pounds, and my family started to worry about my health.

I did eventually yield to the wisdom of allowing myself the rest I needed and put some weight back on. But this concept of disciplined rest (i.e., staying in tune with my body's needs to recover after expending its energy reserves) eluded me after receiving my black belt, and I paid dearly for it.

8. *Winning, losing, and healing.*

Suspense novelist James Patterson once wrote a book entitled *Miracle on the 17th Green*. In the only golf story he has ever written, Patterson's character, Travis McKinley, wins after a series of setbacks in his life. Of his achievement, McKinley says that he finally felt not like he was better than anyone else but just as good. And that while it's okay to believe that "it's not whether you win or lose, it's how you play that counts most," you've got to win one every once in a while. This is because, as he puts it, "people really suck at consoling themselves."

I'll comment more on Patterson's character in this novel later, but the point I want to make here involves the themes of persistence and taking risks. Here's a guy who kept getting kicked in the ass throughout his life—but he continued striving to succeed in something, anything, to prove that he didn't have to resign himself to his unhappy circumstances. He eventually wins, and this helps reassure himself that he was on the right track.

Many people shy away from challenges for fear of failing. They say to themselves in effect, "Hey, you can't lose if you don't try." McKinley fashions his life around this form of self-protection. Unfortunately, the same fortress he built around himself in the service of self-preservation becomes his own self-imposed prison. It nearly chokes the life out of him. At some point, however, he gets so disgusted with himself that he takes a shot at qualifying for the Senior PGA Tour. He exposes himself outside his protective shell in a move that said, "Yeah? Well, you can't *win* if you don't try either."

At the beginning of this book, I recounted Vince Lombardi's credo, "Winning isn't everything, but striving to win is." Beyond preparing yourself well, part of striving to win involves a basic willingness to risk losing. McKinley's win—and with it his own redemption—comes when he puts himself in the position to lose.

7. *Overidentifying with your performance is dangerous to your self-esteem.*

Countless people suffer with the same distorted way of thinking that Patterson's character endured for so many years. When McKinley failed at something he tried, in his mind he became a *failure*. In his career, marriage, and his golf game, he didn't just lose, he was a *loser*.

This same distortion can happen in reverse as well. You can overestimate your importance after winning an award, a game, or a business contract. In either direction, hinging your self-worth or ego on performance outcomes can cause you to put too much pressure on yourself and to lose a proper perspective.

Ego-driven performers tend to judge every incident within their event as it relates to the bottom line—the end result. Consequently, their morale rises and falls based on their perceived chances of winning or losing, succeeding or failing. Besides riding mercilessly on an emotional roller coaster during performances, these folks focus too much on the wrong things and ironically can cause the very outcome they fear most.

During a performance, you must simultaneously process and react well to events as they unfold moment to moment. If you try to do that and deliberate over things that already occurred or that might happen, this gums up the fluidity of your performance. By overloading your mind with past or future errors, you cannot process what's happening now or decide the appropriate response as quickly or efficiently.

During the time that I have written this book, I have watched our New England Patriots football team win the Super Bowl three times. The camera guys seem to like catching Head Coach Bill Belichik patrolling the sidelines during games. An emotional sphinx, you can hardly tell by watching him whether quarterback Tom Brady has thrown a touchdown or an interception.

Belichik appears to have mastered the art of letting go of even the immediate past and instead focusing on the next best strategy given his team's present circumstances. If you only have thirty seconds to get the next play off, you can't waste twenty of them celebrating or lamenting what already happened and is completely beyond your control.

This task-driven approach to performing came into play so often during my black belt test. At times when I got confused and made mistakes, I only made things worse when I worried about what Joe would think or if I might fail. The quicker I accepted the reality of events—with a mind uncluttered by ego-driven regrets or hubris—the easier it became for me to shift to what I needed to do next. So strangely enough, when I let go of my desire to look good to others, that's when I tended to perform my best.

6. *Center yourself.*

Toward the last point, I found that my breathing became the simplest way for me to shift away from my ego concerns and into the present moment. When my mental chatter started to get the best of me in or out of the dojo, I only needed a moment to focus on loosening my jaw and shoulders and lowering the center of my breath. The lower it became, the more grounded I felt—and the easier it became for me to make sounder decisions about what I should do next.

With the practice of centering comes the acceptance of the mind's occasionally turbulent thought patterns. These worries come from some unconscious place and sweep across our conscious mind like gusts of wind that disturb an otherwise serene mountain lake. The stillness of the mind doesn't return, however, by trying to vigorously suppress or struggle with your concerns. That would be like trying to eliminate these gusts by sending wind from the opposing direction. Try telling yourself not to think something, and—*poof*—there it pops back into your mind as strong as ever.

Instead, you need to show patience with yourself. Respect the fact that your mind only tries to warn you of possible dangers—sometimes real, sometimes imagined—and gently reassure yourself that everything will turn out okay. Remind yourself to focus on the safety of the present moment and trust that in doing so, the wind will die down all by itself.

I still practice centering myself several times daily; and I teach it to my clients, family, and friends.

5. *The path of discipline is a path of learning.*

Most people consider the word "discipline" as synonymous with hardship and suffering. They might see this pain as a necessary sacrifice that they must pay to achieve a specific outcome. Unfortunately, this viewpoint has several negative consequences. Namely, adults preaching the need for discipline to kids will have a tough sell. After all, people generally shy away from the notion of a life filled with discomfort and drudgery.

The second problem with this view of discipline involves the idea of hard work as merely an unavoidable means to a desirable goal. This implies that the work itself has no inherent value or pleasure. Perhaps by adopting the puritanical belief that we cannot enjoy work, folks with this attitude take satisfaction only in the rewards that their efforts ultimately yield: a paycheck, a trophy, or a promotion.

Yet the triumphant glow of such rewards fades all too quickly—leaving the recipient no choice but to return to the grindstone for another round of misery. Presumably, this gets endured for a certain period of time until they can once again enjoy their payday. That so many people spend their lives pining for their weekends, vacations, or paychecks seems like such a waste of their limited time here on this planet.

At the root of discipline lies the word "disciple," which means "student." So for me, pursuing a disciplined life means the continual process of learning through deliberate training. This sounds funny for me to say, because for so long I simply *endured* school as a kid. Even the grades meant less to me. That went on until I caught a spark in my learning about this thing called psychology—something I found interesting all by itself. Once determined to become a psychologist, nobody had to prod me to do the work. I devoured the material given to me and got the best grades of my life.

The same could be said of my martial arts training. Even though I have not had to prepare for any tests or competitions since 2000, I look forward to my workouts. I've stayed flexible and fit, and I vary my training regimen to keep from getting bored. I do all this not for any rewards or praise, but because it is now in my blood. I enjoy the process and the way it makes me feel in the moment.

4. *The impact of a mentor cannot be measured.*

The rich legacy of the martial arts would not exist without the countless masters who passed on their skills to the next generation of students. Over time, the line between teacher and student grows blurrier as teachers tend to draw more and more lessons from their own proteges.

Yet mentors can also inflict great harm upon those in their charge. Of course, those exposed to such abuse run the risk of passing that legacy on as well. For better or worse, then, the impact of a teacher may last indefinitely.

Similarly, I've seen the relationship between teacher-and-student breakup over differences in how the next generation wants to carry on the teachings of their mentor. "He was like a second father to me," I recall my first instructor, Master Mezerewski, telling me sadly as he recounted how he and his teacher parted ways. Although entirely capable of running his own school, he ached for the connection he had lost when his former mentor severed their ties.

In his poignant memoir *My Losing Season*, Pat Conroy recalls his painful boyhood growing up with a brutally abusive father. Sadly, just when Conroy frees himself from his father's oppression by going to college, he lands into similar circumstances at the Citadel, an academy for the U.S. Marine Corps. He endures severe hazing as a first-year cadet, and his basketball coach eerily replicates his father's emotional torture.

But Conroy, like so many other resilient kids who rise above their chaotic circumstances, found a charismatic adult to take him under his wing. Having the good fortune of a bright intellect and a gift at writing, his English professor, Colonel John Doyle, took a special liking to Conroy. In the years after his graduating from the Citadel, Conroy kept in contact with this instructor even after his retirement from teaching. At one point, Conroy, now a best-selling author, calls Colonel Doyle, and they share a touching exchange of their mutual affection and respect for each other.

"Thanks for finding me when I was a boy," he tells his longtime friend and mentor, and to which Colonel Doyle retorts, "No no no, Mr. Conroy, you always get that part wrong—we found each other . . . we found each other."

Conroy's story highlights the vital importance of having someone to look up to, someone after whom you can model yourself. If you don't currently have a mentor, find one. If your mentor isn't perfect but has something valuable to say, try to eat around the bad parts—but don't let anyone, not even a mentor, put you down.

I've sought the counsel of mentors my whole life. Perhaps due to my fortunate experience of living in a stable family with good parents, I've had the knack of finding some great ones. They've steadied my ship in rough seas and served as my lighthouse to guide my decisions. In return, I'd like to think they've gotten something back from our times together—perhaps at least in knowing that the people who now seek *my* counsel can reap the benefit of their insights and, at key times, soothing words.

3. *Let go of that which you cannot control.*

Alcoholics Anonymous, the self-help organization for addicts, advocates its members to live by the Serenity Prayer. The prayer goes something like, "God, grant me the serenity to accept the things I cannot change, the courage to change the things I can, and the wisdom to know the difference."

In practice, this can be hard to do, because we tend to fret over many things over which we have little or no control. This might include the economy, weather, past events, and other people's actions or attitudes. It takes courage to stop pointing our finger at all the bad things that life has done to us and to take responsibility for how we respond to them. By staring only at things we can't control, we only feel more powerless.

I couldn't control whether Joe would approve of my performance during Hell Week. And while I admit that this concern hovered around my consciousness, my freedom came when I let it go—when I focused instead on trusting that my body *knew* what to do. This lifted the burden of the future off my shoulders and let me stay in the present. Only then could I fly through the air into balanced stances and bring about the outcome I desired.

2. Bujutsu—*the way of the peaceful warrior.*

At the beginning of this book, I said I wanted to explore, among other things, the themes of violence and conflict. As a sensitive, peace-loving little boy, I learned fairly quickly that not everyone wanted to get along. And in fact, some people seemed to even get some kind of perverse kick out of hurting others—giving little attention to the crippling effects this can have on their victims.

Having skin as soft as a baby's, I deeply felt the pain of a bully's fists and words, along with the hot stinging tears that streamed down my plump young cheeks. Faced with the choice of victimization or standing my ground, I eventually learned how to fight back. At first, it happened when I fought so hard for my life in the middle of Spring Pond. Then it happened within sports in my backyard with my dad and later on the basketball court. And still later, I fought to get ahead in school and in the business world.

Repeatedly overcoming challenges in these various settings had a cumulative healing effect for me. Taken together, these empowering experiences built a reservoir of faith in myself—restoring a basic self-trust that I had lost on the playground as a younger boy. Strangely, my own martial arts training, which started when I was twenty-seven, came almost as a postscript to the evolution of my personal self-confidence and fighting spirit.

The Japanese differentiates between two fundamental approaches in martial training. "Budo" refers to type of training specifically designed for use in actual combat situations you might expect to face. In contrast, practitioners of *Bujutsu* draw from the discipline, conditioning, and focus that comes from the martial arts—with less direct attention on the application of deadly skills *outside* of the dojo.

With all due respect owed to the many soldiers who defend us (and thereby give us the freedom to choose our path), I clearly align with the latter approach. While I'm now able to fend off physical attacks, it's no coincidence that I've never had to use my fighting skills outside of class (and I hope I never will).

The Dalai Lama teaches, "Violence can betray even the noblest of causes." I have found that knowing that I *can* fight paradoxically frees me from the paralyzing fear of getting seriously hurt. This, of course, enables me to think more calmly and flexibly about my nonviolent options (which, in my view, are almost always preferable). In effect, my martial training empowers me to truly *choose* (i.e., not because I *can't* fight) to walk the peaceful path wherever possible.

1. *Connection and connectedness.*

Author Dr. Steven Covey has proposed, "The deepest hunger of the human soul is to be understood." A powerful statement, as it underscores the importance we place on having someone who cares enough about us to listen and understand our feelings. When I meet clients for the first time, I look for evidence of their sense of feeling disconnected in some aspect of their lives. And I listen carefully so that I might offer them a chance to feel connected in my office as they unburden their hearts.

Scientists point to the undeniable connections we have with our universe—that the stars made the planets and that the planet Earth made us. As former vice president Al Gore notes this in his book, *Earth in the Balance*, our bodies share the same ratio of liquids to solids as the Earth—and our blood has the same saline content as the ocean. Similarly, Albert Einstein saw everything around us as the same star matter—only packaged with varying densities of atomic energy.

After killing a buffalo, our own American Indians used to give thanks to their four-legged brothers for giving their lives so that they may have food and clothing. They took nothing for granted when it came to living peacefully with their surroundings, because they saw themselves as part of the same family—born of Mother Earth and Father Sky.

In our present culture, we too often overemphasize the importance of our differences within our human family—racial, cultural, or religious—and fail to acknowledge our common needs and interests. People become objects whom we judge as similar or different or useful or useless to us.

Herein lies the danger that comes when we pass hasty judgments and objectify another group of people: it's too easy to inflict harm on them, because as objects, they no longer seem *human*. Instead, they become Jews, Americans, Arabs, Hispanics, gays, or company management. And then we risk losing our humanity—history shows us this time and again.

On September 11, 2001, I sat in my office with my clients, and we shared our fears and grief. In all my years of practice, I can scarcely think of a time when I felt more connected with my clients. As the events of the day sank in, we spoke of our species as a huge family. Since our country holds a parental role in this world, some angry adolescent had just lashed out against us. And tragically, like most adolescents, he didn't hate our country as much as he did our wealth and power.

The call to strike back came from everywhere, and for a brief while, we had the entire world's sympathies. We did strike back again and again—and so did they in the form of snipers and suicide bombings. But as the fighting continues, we have gotten ourselves into a nasty war with a faceless enemy. And the world has become less and less sympathetic.

So how do we extricate ourselves from this spiral of violence? The key will come through the recognition of our *connectedness*—our mutual needs for safety, food, and upward mobility—instead of fighting over our differences or past injustices. Once every country sees it in their best interest to cooperate with all nations across the world, then we will have a chance for harmony in our human family.

* * *

Author's Postscript

I find it important to add one final thought on the subject of self-improvement—that the merit of our endeavors relates with the value they bring to others' lives. What the Buddhists call "right intention" refers to the need to recognize the dysfunction of succeeding when it entails harming others. Similarly, personal achievement just for the record books may ring hollow if nobody else can benefit from such accomplishments. In the case of earning a black belt, this means perhaps using your martial skills to protect someone from danger. But it also means sharing the wisdom and teachings acquired from mentors with those students that follow you on the black belt path.

Acknowledgements

I want to thank the following people:

My karate teacher and friend, Grand Master Joe Esposito—now a tenth-degree black belt—for his faith in my ability to one day become a black belt and for his extraordinary support throughout the writing of this manuscript (GITFO!). Over the past several years, he granted me access to his experiences, perspectives, and groundbreaking permission to candidly share what happens behind his karate dojo doors. This book simply could not have been written without him.

My wife Pilar, for her continuous support during my martial arts training—especially the black belt test—and for her tolerance for my late-night plunking away at the keyboard completing this book while she tried to sleep.

My friends, fellow students, especially Dave, Dan, and Steven, and all the black belt teachers who gave their time and support over the years.

And my colleagues, especially Dan Kirschenbaum, Glen Ross, Don "Woody" Worden, and Arnie Scheller, who proofread segments of this manuscript—all of whom basically hounded me to complete it.

Suggested Reading

Boukreev, Anatoli, and G. Weston Dewalt. *Climb: Tragic Ambitions on Everest.* St. Martin's Press, 1997.

Conroy, Pat. *My Losing Season: The Point Guard's Way to Knowledge.* Bantam Books, 2003.

Csikszentmihaly, Mihaly. *Flow: The Psychology of Optimal Experience.* HarperPerennial Books, 1990.

Dobson, Terry, and Victor Miller. *Aikido in Everyday Life: Giving in to Get Your Way.* N. Atlantic Books, 1993.

Easterbrook, Gregg. *The Progress Paradox: How Life Gets Better and People Feel Worse.* Random House Adult Trade Publishing Group, 2004.

Gore, Al. *Earth in the Balance: Ecology and the Human Spirit.* Rodale Press, 2006.

Herrigel, Eugen. *Zen in the Art of Archery.* Vintage Books, 1971.

Himes, Michael. *Doing the Truth in Love: Conversations about God, Relationships and Service.* Paulist Press, 1995.

Hyams, Joe. *Zen in the Martial Arts.* Bantam Books, 1982.

Jackson, Phil. *Sacred Hoops: Spiritual Lessons a Hardwood Warrior.* Hyperion Books, 1995.

Jacob, Rob. *Martial arts biographies: An annotated bibliography.* iUniverse, Inc. 2005.

Krakauer Jon. *Into Thin Air: A personal Account of the Mt. Everest Disaster.* Anchor Books, 1997.

Lee, Bruce. *The Tao of Jeet Kun Do.* Black Belt Communications, 1975.

Leonard, George. *Mastery: The Keys to Success and Long Term Fulfillment.* Plume Books, 1991.

Lowery, David. *Autumn Lighting: The Education of an American Samurai.* Shambhala Publications, 1999.

Mahony, John. *The Tao of the Jumpshot: An Eastern Approach to Life and Basketball.* Seastone Books, 1999.

Millman, Dan. *The Way of the Peaceful Warrior: A book that Changes Lives.* New World Library, 2000.

Morgan, Maj. Forest. *Living the Martial Way: A Manual for the Way a Modern Warriror Should Think.* Barricade Books, 1992.

Patterson, James, and Peter De Jonge. *Miracle on the Seventeenth Green.* Little, Brown, and Company, 1999.

Salzman, Mark. *Lost in Place: Growing up Absurd in Suburbia.* Random House Books, 1995.

Schwartz, Barry. *The Paradox of Choice: Why More Is Less.* HarperCollins, 2005.

Shoemaker, Fred, and Pete Shoemaker. *Extraordinary Golf: The Art of the Possible.* Perigee Books, 1996.

Tolle, Eckart. *The Power of Now: A Guide to Spiritual Enlightenment.* New World Library, 1999.

About the Author

Dr. Rob Smith is a licensed clinical psychologist and a certified consultant of the Association for the Advancement of Applied Sport Psychology. He serves on the U. S. Olympic Committee's Registry of Sport Psychologists. A specialist in performance enhancement, Dr. Smith has helped thousands of people make important changes in their lives through his workshops and consulting services. He has written numerous articles for newspapers, magazines, and professional journals, and co-wrote a chapter for a popular sport psychology textbook. He has spoken at conferences internationally, and has appeared on local and national television and radio shows. His website is www.ShootingForSuccess.com.